ESSENTIAL BIBLIOGRAPHY OF AMERICAN FICTION

MODERN CLASSIC WRITERS

Matthew J. Bruccoli and
Judith S. Baughman,
Series Editors

Foreword by George Garrett

Facts On File®

AN INFOBASE HOLDINGS COMPANY

MODERN CLASSIC WRITERS

Copyright © 1994 by Manly, Inc. and Facts On File, Inc.

Facts On File, Inc.
460 Park Avenue South
New York NY 10016

Library of Congress Cataloging-in-Publication Data
Modern classic writers / Matthew J. Bruccoli and Judith S. Baughman,
    series editors; foreword by George Garrett.
        p. cm. — (Essential bibliography of American fiction)
    Includes bibliographical references (p.) and index.
    ISBN 0-8160-3002-2 (alk. paper).— ISBN 0-8160-3003-0 (pbk.:
    alk. paper)
    1. American fiction—20th century—History and criticism—
    Bibliography. 2. American fiction—20th century—Bibliography.
    I. Bruccoli, Matthew Joseph, 1931- . II. Baughman, Judith,
    III. Series.
    Z1231.F4M63 1993
    [PS379]
    016.813'509—dc20   93-8641

A British CIP catalogue record for this book is available from the British Library.

Facts On File books are available at special discounts when purchased in bulk quantities for businesses, associations, institutions or sales promotions. Please call our Special Sales Department in New York at 212/683-2244 or 800/322-8755.

Text design by Catherine Hyman
Cover design by Heidi Haeuser
Composition by Grace M. Ferrara/Facts On File, Inc.
Manufactured by the Maple-Vail Book Manufacturing Group

Printed in the United States of America

10 9 8 7 6 5 4 3 2 1

This book is printed on acid-free paper.

CONTENTS

SERIES INTRODUCTION

These volumes in the *Essential Bibliography of American Fiction* series are largely adapted from author entries in *Facts On File Bibliography of American Fiction, 1919–1988* (1991) and *Facts On File Bibliography of American Fiction, 1866–1918* (1993), known as *BAF*. The *Essential Bibliography of American Fiction* makes *BAF* material on certain widely read and widely studied authors available in a more affordable format. Whereas *BAF* is intended for colleges and university research libraries, the *Essential Bibliography of American Fiction* volumes are revised for high schools, community colleges and general libraries—as well as for classroom use.

None of the author entries in this new series is a direct reprint from *BAF*. Each entry has been updated to the end of 1992. The primary bibliographies are complete, but the secondary bibliographies have been trimmed. The *Essential Bibliography of American Fiction* entries are modified for general usability by a cross-section of students, teachers and serious readers. Asterisks now identify the most generally available and most influential secondary books and articles. The asterisks do not designate the best works—which is a matter for argument; the asterisks mark what can be described as "standard" biographical and critical works.

To enhance the usefulness of the *Essential Bibliography of American Fiction,* new entries have been compiled for authors who are not in *BAF*—notably writers born after 1940.

The authors in each *Essential Bibliography of American Fiction* volume are eminent fiction writers who have been grouped on the basis of their backgrounds and materials. The selection of the figures was made in consultation with teachers and librarians. Since a writer will appear in only one volume, it was necessary to decide in which of several possible volumes a figure should be placed: Toni Morrison, for example, was assigned to *Modern African American Writers* rather than to *Modern Women Writers.*

Mark Twain declared that ". . . almost the most prodigious asset of a country, and perhaps its most precious possession, is its native literary product—when that product is free and noble and enduring." The power of literature requires collaboration between authors and their readers. The *Essential Bibliography of American Fiction* series endeavors to promote that collaboration.

FOREWORD

It is very hard to imagine the world without the writers represented in this book. They are now in place, a gigantic brooding presence, casting huge shadows like the Rocky Mountains, not only in literature, our *world* literature, but also in the society we live in. It is a society they set out to describe accurately and honestly (which is why we call them "social realists") and ended up by helping to shape. Much of our own mindset, the way we look at things, think about things, and, above all, the way that we *feel* about things, has been profoundly influenced by their art and the vision behind it. No writer anywhere in the world can really ignore or escape their lasting influence. The idea of what constitutes what we now crudely call "creative writing" comes from them and their example; and, for better or worse, they created the idea and the image of what it means to be a writer.

It is even harder, then to try to *reimagine* the world they were born into and in which they grew up—the world before their generation. Of course, in the beginning it was *not* the whole world, not one world. It was the United States of America, separated from both Europe and Asia by thousands of miles of ocean and even more separate in its desire not to be involved in the life and times of "the Old World." It was, in a word, provincial, distant from and mostly indifferent to the sophisticated cultural capitals of foreign countries. Our nation was, as well, distant and different from the way it is now. Still healing from our own Civil War, which was, in a relative sense, the most bloody and terrible of the modern wars, before or since, the United States was a world we might not easily recognize. It was still a mostly rural country, wide and spacious, with large parts of the West only thinly settled. Most people alive at the end of the last century and the beginning of the twentieth were destined not to travel more than, maybe, fifty miles from the place where they were born. Not only the wide world, but also the rest of the United States was distant and mysterious to them. Outside of the great cities electricity and running water ("indoor plumbing") were rare. Phones were few and new. Radio was coming one of these days. Television was a science fiction dream. (It was still a sort of fantastic novelty, something for the distant future, as late as the 1939 World's Fair in New York where some primitive sets were displayed.) Into this generation came the automobile, the airplane, the motion picture. Even the photograph, though not new, was unusual. The illustrations in most newspapers and magazines, for example, were mostly drawings.

So, the first thing that happened to our writers was that the world their parents knew was on fire with change. Everything, large and small, seemed to be changing and nobody could foresee the future or guess whether the multitudinous changes were for good or ill.

It might have been enough to stun this new generation into cautious silence. How could they manage to describe a reality that was changing shape and substance even as they looked at it? It seemed impossible; yet it was this burning sense of change that gave each of these writers, as different as they are from each other, a basic subject matter—the continual clash between old and new.

One huge change was that America joined the world, inescapably, when this nation despite its best intentions (and the promises of leaders) found itself involved in World War I—which sent hundreds of thousands of young Americans overseas to fight and sent millions all across the United States to training camps from everywhere, far and near. From that time forward, encouraged by the new ways and means of transportation, the American population would be gradually, but more and more, nomadic, freely mobile. By the end of that war, America was awake to the rest of the world and to itself. Some of the writers we are talking about served in that war and some witnessed events of it at first hand. But whether they went to it or not, it was part of their experience. The veterans of World War I were all around them. Their stories were common currency.

When these American writers set out to write their fiction, they seldom had any kind of literary program or theory except this—they had been so shocked and energized by all that was new and different (and often dangerous) that they were convinced that neither the language nor the forms of storytelling of the past could work any more to tell the truth of things. They wanted to tell the truth. They were seeking originality, in the best sense of the word, working with diligence and dedication to find new ways to tell true stories in a language that was alive and authentic. In a serious sense, the British and European writers all sounded somewhat alike; for essentially they had all enjoyed a similar education with the same basic cultural literacy at the heart of it. For these Americans there were more differences than likenesses among them. Individuality was their ideal. And they had turned to the riches of the American language, especially its culturally diverse vernacular, to create a style that could capture the reality of American life. Some of them offered (among other things) not a revision, but a new vision of the past. This is one of William Faulkner's great subjects. Thomas Wolfe did the same thing with personal history, constantly rewriting and revising his own life until it became larger than itself, more representative; F. Scott Fitzgerald, Sinclair Lewis and John O'Hara, each differently in his own distinctive style, labored to seize the present moment, to tell us *how we are* at the moment of their writing. John Steinbeck was deeply concerned, as was John Dos Passos, about the enormous impact of historical and social forces on individuals. Ernest Hemingway, in his clean, clear, evocative style, sought to isolate the purity of the present without benefit of past or future. What he succeeded in doing was to create a standard of intense immediacy that can compete with that of the finest photographs or moving pictures.

As different as these master artists are from each other—and most of the time each has a style so personal that the reader cannot easily confuse them—they all share an intense interest in and respect for details, for the *facts* of life. In one of his earliest poems, "Mowing," written at roughly the same time these writers were arriving at maturity, Robert Frost said: "The fact is the sweetest dream that labor knows." The work of these artists demonstrates that they felt much the same way. The first step toward understanding the truth was to get the facts right, to record details accurately. They did not set out to be anything more (or less) than American storytellers, certainly not social historians. Yet that is what they became, looking back to record the old world even as it faded away, looking ahead to a new world as it gradually came into focus and perspective. To do this, they needed some solid ground to stand on—home bases. Thus we have, for example, Thomas Wolfe's Altamont and William Faulkner's Yoknapatawpha County. For others, like Fitzgerald, Hemingway, and Dos Passos, there were multiple places at home and abroad; and the search for stability, for some kind of solid ground, became a major theme for them.

All of these writers came out of the American middle class and all were townsmen, at once uprooted and set free by the forces of the new century. Drawing their inspiration and their language from the way people really talked, formally and informally, to each other, from the ways people lived and thought and acted, influenced by everything—by our great modernist poets and artists, by the newspapers, even the funny papers—these writers changed not just American literature, but world literature completely from then to now. Every reader and writer since them is beholden to them.

Here, then, is the record of their life's work, not merely a demonstration of great achievement, but, more to the point, an invitation to enter their world and to experience it.

> —*George Garrett*
> Hoyns Professor of Creative Writing
> The University of Virginia

USING THE *ESSENTIAL BIBLIOGRAPHY OF AMERICAN FICTION*

T he only basis for the full understanding and proper judgment of any author is what the writer wrote. To grasp the significance and value of a literary career, it is necessary to have a sense of the author's body of work. Bibliographies—lists of what the author wrote and what has been published about the author and the author's work—are the crucial tools of literary study.

The reader should always begin with the *primary* bibliography (the list of books *by* the author). What the author wrote is always much more important than what has been written about the works. Everything comes from the works themselves. Great fiction is much more than plot or story. The capacity of literature to move, excite, or gratify the reader results from the writing itself. Every great writer writes like no one else.

Yet writings about a work of literature may enlarge the reader's understanding. There is a point in the study of literature when the reader—in or out of the classroom—needs the help provided by sound, usable scholarship. Criticism varies greatly in its sense and utility. The best critics act as trustworthy intermediaries between the work and the reader, but the reader has the right to reject unhelpful critical material.

After reading the story or novel, the researcher should first consult a comprehensive bibliography of writings about the author's life and work— as cited in the *Essential Bibliography of American Fiction (EBAF)*. An annotated secondary bibliography will provide brief indications of the content of articles and books. Thus a student seeking sources for a critical analysis of Ernest Hemingway's "Big Two-Hearted River" should check Hanneman's *Ernest Hemingway: A Comprehensive Bibliography* and its *Supplement,* which describe thirteen articles and book sections dealing with this story up to 1974. An easy way to start is to check the *EBAF* Hemingway items against Hanneman. The annotations in Hanneman should aid the researcher to identify those items with the strongest interest or utility for that researcher.

Researchers without access to the Hanneman volumes—which are not available in small libraries—should consult *EBAF* to find other basic reference tools: for example, Wagner's *Ernest Hemingway: A Reference Guide* and Larson's *Ernest Hemingway: A Reference Guide, 1974–1989,* both of which are annotated. A student working on a particular story would consult the lists of sources in the books about Hemingway's short fiction: for example, Smith's *A Reader's Guide to the Short Stories of Ernest Hemingway*.

Literary biography is not a substitute for the works, but biography augments the understanding of individual works and their function in the author's total achievement. Dr. Samuel Johnson, the great eighteenth-century literary biographer, observed that just as a soldier's life proceeds from battle to battle, so does a writer's life proceed from book to book. The more the reader knows about the writer, the more fully the reader will recognize the material for the fictions.

The author entries in *EBAF* provide guides for extended study of each writer's life and work; that is, they function as tutors for lifetime reading. Knowledge propagates knowledge. All literary activity is a process of discovery. In literary study it is crucial that students connect what they are reading with what they have previously read. Willing readers and students have been impeded by the inability to find out what to read next—or where to look for the answers to their questions. Reference books are portable universities. The *Essential Bibliography of American Fiction* provides keys to reference tools, organized according to the writers who secured the genius of American fiction.

PLAN OF THE ENTRIES

All authors selected for the *Essential Bibliography of American Fiction* receive the same treatment. No attempt has been made to indicate the stature of an author by the form of the entry. The length and scope of each entry is determined by the author's career.

The brief headnotes on the entries place the authors in terms of their reputations in their own time and now.

The first section of each author entry is reserved for BIBLIOGRAPHIES. Author bibliographies are traditionally divided into *primary works* (by the author) and *secondary works* (about the author).

The PRIMARY MATERIAL list in each entry begins with all BOOKS written by the subject author, as well as books for which the author had a major responsibility (as a collaborator or a ghost-writer). The next primary section includes LETTERS, DIARIES, NOTEBOOKS and is usually restricted to book-length works. The third primary section, OTHER, includes volumes in which the subject author was involved as contributor, editor, or translator; this list is selective. The final primary section, EDITIONS & COLLECTIONS, includes standard one-volume gatherings and multi-volume editions.

The MANUSCRIPTS & ARCHIVES section identifies the principal holdings of the author's manuscripts, typescripts, letters, and private papers in libraries or other institutional repositories.

A CONCORDANCE is an index of the words in a work or works by an author. Concordances are irreplaceable tools for the study of style and imagery.

The BIOGRAPHIES section is divided into three parts: *Books, Book Sections,* and *Articles* that focus on the author's career rather than on assessments of his or her work. This section is usually followed by INTERVIEWS, which includes book-length collections of interviews and single interviews of special interest.

The section of CRITICAL STUDIES is divided into five parts:
1. *Critical Books*;
2. Book-length *Collections of Essays* by various critics on the author or a single work by that author;
3. *Special Journals* devoted to an author (*Hemingway Review, Flannery O'Connor Bulletin*), as well as single issues of general scholarly journals (*Modern Fiction Studies*) dealing with that author;
4. *Book Sections* of volumes that treat several authors;
5. Journal or newspaper *Articles* that are critical rather than biographical.

In selecting articles, the contributors and editors have kept the resources and requirements of smaller libraries in mind. However, the most influential articles are always included.

TABLE OF ABBREVIATIONS

& c = and other cities
ed = editor or edited by
et al = and others
nd = no date provided
no = number
nos = numbers
Npl = no place of publication provided in the work
npub = no publisher provided in the work
ns = new series
P = Press
passim = throughout the volume
pp = pages
Repub = republished
Rev = revised
Rpt = reprinted
Sect = Section
U = University
U P = University Press
Vol = volume

The following acronyms are the actual titles of journals:

CLIO
ELH
MELUS
PMLA

WILLIAM FAULKNER
New Albany, Miss, 25 Sep 1897–Oxford, Miss, 2 Jul 1962

William Faulkner is acknowledged as one of the most innovative novelists of the twentieth century. Faulkner's commercial success came slowly, though his critical reputation was firmly established with four remarkable psychological novels published between 1929 and 1933: *The Sound and the Fury, As I Lay Dying, Sanctuary,* and *Light in August.* Despite tours of what he considered purely commercial labor as a Hollywood scriptwriter during the 1930s and 1940s, Faulkner, in the 1950s, finished his "Magnum O," the controversial *A Fable,* as well as the final two volumes of the Snopes trilogy. In 1950, as his reputation rose, Faulkner received the Nobel Prize. It has been said that, among authors in English, only Shakespeare receives more written attention than Faulkner. The result is a bewildering amount of criticism, most of which celebrates his literary impact. Faulkner's works have fared best, however, under the scrutiny of investigators who study the styles, structures, and fictional world of his canon.

Bibliographies & Catalogues

American Literary Scholarship: An Annual, 1963– . Durham, NC: Duke U P, 1965– . Chapters on WF.

Bassett, John. *WF: An Annotated Checklist of Criticism.* NY: Lewis, 1972.

Bassett. *F: An Annotated Checklist of Recent Criticism.* Kent, Ohio: Kent State U P, 1983.

Bassett. *F in the Eighties: An Annotated Critical Bibliography.* Metuchen, NJ: Scarecrow, 1991. Secondary.

Blotner, Joseph. *WF's Library: A Catalogue.* Charlottesville: U P Virginia, 1964.

Brodsky, Louis D & Robert W Hamblin. *F: A Comprehensive Guide to the Brodsky Collection,* Vols 1–5. Jackson: U P Mississippi, 1982–1988. Catalogue of primary & secondary materials. Includes texts of previously unpublished material.

*Cox, Leland H. *WF: Biographical and Reference Guide*. Detroit: Gale, 1982. Primary & secondary.

Kinney, Arthur F & Doreen Fowler. "F's Rowan Oak Papers: A Census." *Journal of Modern Literature*, 10 (Jun 1983), 327–334. Primary.

Massey, Linton. *"Man Working," 1919–1962: WF: A Catalogue of the WF Collections at the University of Virginia*. Charlottesville: Bibliographical Society, U Virginia, 1968. Primary & secondary.

*McHaney, Thomas L. *WF: A Reference Guide*. Boston: Hall, 1976. Secondary.

*Meriwether, James B. *The Literary Career of WF: A Bibliographical Study*. Princeton: Princeton U P, 1961. Repub, Columbia: U South Carolina P, 1971. Primary.

*Meriwether. "The Books of WF: A Revised Guide for Students and Scholars." *Mississippi Quarterly*, 35 (Summer 1982), 265–281. Rpt Cox, *WF: Critical Collection*. Primary.

Price-Stephens, Gordon. "The British Reception of WF, 1929–1962." *Mississippi Quarterly*, 18 (Summer 1965), 119–200. Secondary.

Sensibar, Judith L, with the assistance of Nancy L Stegall. *F's Poetry: A Bibliographic Guide to Texts and Criticism*. Ann Arbor, Mich: UMI, 1988. Primary & secondary.

Skei, Hans. *WF: The Short Story Career: An Outline of F's Short Story Writing From 1919 to 1962*. Oslo: Universitetsforlaget, 1981. Primary & secondary.

Books

The Marble Faun. Boston: Four Seas, 1924. Poems.

Soldiers' Pay. NY: Boni & Liveright, 1926. Novel.

Mosquitoes. NY: Boni & Liveright, 1927. Novel.

Sartoris. NY: Harcourt, Brace, 1929. Novel.

The Sound and the Fury. NY: Cape & Smith, 1929. Corrected text, ed Noel Polk. NY: Random House, 1984. Novel.

As I Lay Dying. NY: Cape & Smith, 1930. Novel.

Sanctuary. NY: Cape & Smith, 1931. *Sanctuary: The Original Text*, ed Polk. NY: Random House, 1981. Novel.

These 13. NY: Cape & Smith, 1931. Stories.

Idyll in the Desert. NY: Random House, 1931. Story.

Miss Zilphia Gant. Dallas: Book Club of Texas, 1932. Story.

Light in August. NY: Smith & Haas, 1932. Novel.

A Green Bough. NY: Smith & Haas, 1933. Poems.

Doctor Martino and Other Stories. NY: Smith & Haas, 1934.

Pylon. NY: Smith & Haas, 1935. Novel.

Absalom, Absalom! NY: Random House, 1936. Novel.

The Unvanquished. NY: Random House, 1938. Novel.

The Wild Palms. NY: Random House, 1939. Novel.

The Hamlet. NY: Random House, 1940 (Vol 1 of the Snopes trilogy). Novel.

Go Down, Moses. NY: Random House, 1942. Novel.

Intruder in the Dust. NY: Random House, 1948. Novel.

Knight's Gambit. NY: Random House, 1949. Novella & stories.

Collected Stories. NY: Random House, 1950.

Notes on a Horsethief. Greenville, Miss: Levee, 1950. Story.

Requiem for a Nun. NY: Random House, 1951. Novel.

Mirrors of Chartres Street. Minneapolis: Faulkner Studies, 1953. Stories & sketches.

A Fable. NY: Random House, 1954. Novel.

Big Woods. NY: Random House, 1955. Stories.

F's County: Tales of Yoknapatawpha County. London: Chatto & Windus, 1955.

The Town. NY: Random House, 1957 (Vol 2 of the Snopes trilogy). Novel.

New Orleans Sketches, ed Carvel Collins. New Brunswick, NJ: Rutgers U P, 1958. Rev ed, NY: Random House, 1968. Stories, essays & poems.

The Mansion. NY: Random House, 1959 (Vol 3 of the Snopes trilogy). Novel.

The Reivers. NY: Random House, 1962. Novel.

F's University Pieces, ed Collins. Tokyo: Kenkyusha, 1962. Poems, drawings, stories & essays.

Early Prose and Poetry, ed Collins. Boston & Toronto: Atlantic/Little, Brown, 1962. Poems, drawings, stories & essays.

Essays, Speeches, and Public Letters, ed James B Meriwether. NY: Random House, 1965.

The Wishing Tree. NY: Random House, 1967. Children's story.

Flags in the Dust, ed Douglas Day. NY: Random House, 1974. Uncut version of *Sartoris.*

The Marionettes. Charlottesville: U Virginia Library, 1975. Repub, ed Polk. Charlottesville: U P Virginia, 1977. Facsimile of manuscript play.

Mayday. Facsimile of manuscript, Notre Dame, Ind: U Notre Dame P, 1976. Typeset edition, ed Collins. Notre Dame & London: Notre Dame P, 1978. Allegorical prose tale.

Uncollected Stories, ed Joseph Blotner. NY: Random House, 1979.

Mississippi Poems. Oxford, Miss: Yoknapatawpha, 1979. Facsimile of typescript.

The Ghosts of Rowan Oak: WF's Ghost Stories for Children, recounted by Dean Faulkner Wells. Oxford, Miss: Yoknapatawpha, 1980.

To Have and Have Not, with Jules Furthman; ed with intro by Bruce F Kawin. Madison: U Wisconsin P, 1980. Screenplay.

Helen: A Courtship. Facsimile of typescript, New Orleans: Tulane U / Oxford, Miss: Yoknapatawpha, 1981. Typeset edition, *Helen: A Courtship and Mississippi Poems*. New Orleans: Tulane U / Oxford, Miss: Yoknapatawpha, 1981. Poems.

The Road to Glory, with Joel Sayre; afterword by George Garrett. Carbondale & Edwardsville: Southern Illinois U P, 1981. Screenplay.

F's MGM Screenplays, ed Kawin. Knoxville: U Tennessee P, 1982.

Elmer, ed Dianne Cox. Northport, Ala: Seajay, 1983. Novel fragment.

Father Abraham, ed Meriwether. NY: Random House, 1984. Novel fragment.

Vision in Spring, ed Judith Sensibar. Austin: U Texas P, 1984. Poems.

The De Gaulle Story, ed Louis D Brodsky & Robert W Hamblin. Jackson & London: U P Mississippi, 1984 (Vol 3 of *F: A Comprehensive Guide to the Brodsky Collection*). Screenplay.

Battle Cry, ed Brodsky & Hamblin. Jackson & London: U P Mississippi, 1985 (Vol 4 of *F: A Comprehensive Guide to the Brodsky Collection*). Screenplay.

WF Manuscripts, 25 vols, ed Blotner, Thomas L McHaney, Michael Millgate & Polk. NY & London: Garland, 1986–1987.

Country Lawyer and Other Stories for the Screen, ed Brodsky & Hamblin. Jackson & London: U P Mississippi, 1987. Screenplays.

Letters

The F-Cowley File: Letters and Memories, 1944–1962 by Malcolm Cowley. NY: Viking, 1966.

Selected Letters, ed Joseph Blotner. NY: Random House, 1977.

Thinking of Home: WF's Letters to His Mother and Father, 1918–1925, ed James G Watson. NY & London: Norton, 1992.

Other

"Introduction." *Sanctuary* (NY: Modern Library, 1932), v-viii. Rpt *Essays, Speeches, and Public Letters.*

Editions & Collections

The Portable F, ed Malcolm Cowley. NY: Viking, 1946. Rev ed, NY: Viking, 1967; *The Essential F.* London: Chatto & Windus, 1967.

The F Reader. NY: Random House, 1954.

The Collected Stories of WF, 3 vols. London: Chatto & Windus, 1958.

The Marble Faun and A Green Bough. NY: Random House, 1965.

Novels, 1930–1935: As I Lay Dying, Sanctuary, Light in August, Pylon, ed Joseph Blotner & Noel Polk. NY: Library of America, 1985.

Novels, 1936–1940: Absalom, Absalom!, The Unvanquished, If I Forget Thee, Jerusalem [The Wild Palms], The Hamlet, ed Blotner & Polk. NY: Library of America, 1990.

Manuscripts & Archives

The major collections are at the U of Virginia Library; New York Public Library; Harry Ransom Humanities Research Center, U of Texas, Austin; Southeast Missouri State U Library; & U of Mississippi Library.

Concordances

Capps, Jack L. *As I Lay Dying: A Concordance to the Novel.* Ann Arbor, Mich: U Microfilms, 1977.

Capps. *Go Down, Moses: A Concordance to the Novel.* Ann Arbor, Mich: U Microfilms, 1977.

Capps. *Light in August: A Concordance to the Novel,* 2 vols. Ann Arbor, Mich: U Microfilms International, 1979.

Polk, Noel. *Requiem for a Nun: A Concordance to the Novel.* Ann Arbor, Mich: U Microfilms International, 1979.

Polk. *Intruder in the Dust: A Concordance to the Novel.* Ann Arbor, Mich: UMI, 1983.

Polk & John D Hart. *The Mansion: A Concordance to the Novel,* 2 vols. Ann Arbor, Mich: UMI, 1988.

Polk & Hart. *Absalom, Absalom!: A Concordance to the Novel,* 2 vols. Ann Arbor, Mich: UMI, 1989.

Polk & Hart. *Pylon: A Concordance to the Novel.* Ann Arbor, Mich: UMI, 1989.

Polk & Hart. *Collected Stories of WF: Concordances to the Forty-two Short Stories,* 5 vols. Ann Arbor, Mich: UMI, 1990.

Polk & Hart. *The Hamlet: A Concordance to the Novel,* 2 vols. Ann Arbor, Mich: UMI, 1990.

Polk & Hart. *The Reivers: A Concordance to the Novel.* Ann Arbor, Mich: UMI, 1990.

Polk & Hart. *Sanctuary: The Original Text, 1981: A Concordance to the Novel.* Ann Arbor, Mich: UMI, 1990.

Polk & Hart. *Sanctuary: Corrected First Edition Text, Library of America, 1985: A Concordance to the Novel.* Ann Arbor, Mich: UMI, 1990.

Polk & Hart. *Uncollected Stories of WF: Concordances to the Forty-five Short Stories,* 5 vols. Ann Arbor, Mich: UMI, 1990.

Polk & Lawrence Z Pizzi. *The Town: A Concordance to the Novel,* 2 vols. Ann Arbor, Mich: UMI, 1985.

Polk & Kenneth Privratsky. *The Sound and the Fury: A Concordance to the Novel.* Ann Arbor, Mich: Microfilms International, 1980.

Polk & Privratsky. *A Fable: A Concordance to the Novel.* Ann Arbor, Mich: UMI, 1981.

Privratsky. *The Wild Palms: A Concordance to the Novel.* Ann Arbor, Mich: UMI, 1983.

Biographies

BOOKS

Bezzerides, A I. *WF: A Life on Paper,* ed Ann Abadie. Jackson: U P Mississippi, 1980.

Blotner, Joseph. *F: A Biography*, 2 vols. NY: Random House, 1974. * Rev ed, 1 vol. NY: Random House, 1984.

*Cofield, J R. *WF: The Cofield Collection*. Oxford, Miss: Yoknapatawpha, 1978. Pictorial biography.

Falkner, Murry C. *The Fs of Mississippi*. Baton Rouge: Louisiana State U P, 1967.

Faulkner, Jim. *Across the Creek: F Family Stories*. Jackson: U P Mississippi, 1986.

Faulkner, John. *My Brother Bill: An Affectionate Reminiscence*. NY: Trident, 1963.

Gresset, Michel. *A F Chronology,* trans Arthur B Scharff. Jackson: U P Mississippi, 1985.

Minter, David. *WF: His Life and Work*. Baltimore, Md: Johns Hopkins U P, rev 1982.

Snell, Susan. *Phil Stone of Oxford: A Vicarious Life*. Athens: U Georgia P, 1991.

Taylor, Herman E. *F's Oxford: Recollections and Reflections*. Nashville: Rutledge Hills, 1990.

Webb, James W & A Wigfall Green. *WF of Oxford*. Baton Rouge: Louisiana State U P, 1965.

Wilde, Meta Carpenter & Orin Borsten. A *Loving Gentleman: The Love Story of WF and Meta Carpenter*. NY: Simon & Schuster, 1976.

BOOK SECTIONS

Dardis, Tom. "WF: 'They're Gonna Pay Me Saturday, They're Gonna Pay Me Saturday.'" *Some Time in the Sun* (NY: Scribners, 1976), 78–149.

Holditch, W Kenneth. "The Brooding Air of the Past: WF." *Literary New Orleans: Essays and Meditations,* ed Richard S Kennedy (Baton Rouge: Louisiana State U P, 1992), 38–50.

Interviews

BOOKS

Fant, Joseph L & Robert P Ashley, eds. *F at West Point*. NY: Random House, 1964.

*Gwynn, Frederick & Joseph Blotner. *F in the University: Class Conferences at the University of Virginia, 1957–1958*. Charlottesville: U P Virginia, 1959.

*Meriwether, James B & Michael Millgate, eds. *Lion in the Garden: Interviews With WF, 1926–1962*. NY: Random House, 1968.

Critical Studies

BOOKS

*Adams, Richard P. *F: Myth and Motion*. Princeton, NJ: Princeton U P, 1968.

Bleikasten, André. *F's As I Lay Dying,* trans Roger Little. Bloomington: Indiana U P, 1973.

*Bleikasten. *The Most Splendid Failure: F's The Sound and the Fury*. Bloomington: Indiana U P, 1976.

Bleikasten. *The Ink of Melancholy: F's Novels From The Sound and the Fury to Light in August*. Bloomington: Indiana U P, 1990.

*Brooks, Cleanth. *WF: The Yoknapatawpha Country*. New Haven, Conn: Yale U P, 1963.

*Brooks. *WF: Toward Yoknapatawpha and Beyond*. New Haven, Conn: Yale U P, 1978.

*Brown, Calvin S. *A Glossary of F's South*. New Haven, Conn: Yale U P, 1976.

Brylowski, Walter. *F's Olympian Laugh: Myth in the Novels*. Detroit: Wayne State U P, 1968.

Butterworth, Abner Keen. *A Critical and Textual Study of F's A Fable*. Ann Arbor, Mich: UMI, 1983.

Coindreau, Maurice Edgar. *The Time of WF*, ed & trans chiefly by George McMillan Reeves. Columbia: U South Carolina P, 1971.

Creighton, Joanne V. *WF's Craft of Revision*. Detroit: Wayne State U P, 1977.

*Dasher, Thomas E. *WF's Characters: An Index to the Published and Unpublished Fiction*. NY: Garland, 1981.

Davis, Thadious. *F's "Negro": Art and the Southern Context*. Baton Rouge: Louisiana State U P, 1983.

Fadiman, Regina K. *F's Light in August: A Description and Interpretation of the Revisions*. Charlottesville: U P Virginia, 1975.

*Hoffman, Daniel. *F's Country Matters: Folklore and Fable in Yoknapatawpha.* Baton Rouge: Louisiana State U P, 1989.

Hönnighausen, Lothar. *WF: The Art of Stylization in His Early Graphic and Literary Work.* Cambridge: Cambridge U P, 1987.

Hunt, John W. *WF: Art in Theological Tension.* Syracuse, NY: Syracuse U P, 1965.

Irwin, John T. *Doubling and Incest, Repetition and Revenge.* Baltimore, Md: Johns Hopkins U P, 1975.

Kartiganer, Donald M. *The Fragile Thread: The Meaning of Form in F's Novels.* Amherst: U Massachusetts P, 1979.

*Kawin, Bruce. *F and Film.* NY: Ungar, 1977.

Kreiswirth, Martin. *WF: The Making of a Novelist.* Athens: U Georgia P, 1983.

Matthews, John T. *The Play of F's Language.* Ithaca, NY: Cornell U P, 1982.

McHaney, Thomas L. *WF's The Wild Palms.* Jackson: U P Mississippi, 1975.

*Millgate, Michael. *The Achievement of WF.* NY: Random House, 1966. Rpt Lincoln: U Nebrasha P, 1978. Rpt Athens: U Georgia P, 1989.

*Parker, Robert Dale. *Absalom, Absalom!: The Questioning of Fictions.* Boston: Twayne, 1991.

Polk, Noel. *F's Requiem for a Nun: A Critical Study.* Bloomington: Indiana U P, 1981.

Ragan, David Paul. *WF's Absalom, Absalom!: A Critical Study.* Ann Arbor, Mich: UMI, 1987.

Reed, Joseph W, Jr. *F's Narrative.* New Haven, Conn: Yale U P, 1973.

Ross, Stephen M. *Fiction's Inexhaustible Voice: Speech and Writing in F.* Athens: U Georgia P, 1989.

Ruppersburg, Hugh M. *Voice and Eye in F's Fiction.* Athens: U Georgia P, 1983.

*Schoenberg, Estella. *Old Tales and Talking: Quentin Compson in WF's Absalom, Absalom! and Related Works.* Jackson: U P Mississippi, 1977.

Schwartz, Lawrence H. *Creating F's Reputation: The Politics of Modern Literary Criticism.* Knoxville: U Tennessee P, 1988.

Skei, Hans H. *WF: The Short Story Career.* Oslo: Universitetsforlaget, 1981.

*Vickery, Olga. *The Novels of WF: A Critical Interpretation.* Baton Rouge: Louisiana State U P, rev 1964.

Weinstein, Philip M. *F's Subject: A Cosmos No One Owns*. NY: Cambridge U P, 1992.

COLLECTIONS OF ESSAYS

Barth, J Robert, ed. *Religious Perspectives in F's Fiction: Yoknapatawpha and Beyond*. Notre Dame, Ind: U Notre Dame P, 1972.

Bassett, John, ed. *WF: The Critical Heritage*. London: Routledge & Kegan Paul, 1975.

*Bleikasten, André, ed. *WF's The Sound and the Fury: A Critical Casebook*. NY: Garland, 1982.

*Brodhead, Richard H, ed. *F: New Perspectives*. Englewood Cliffs, NJ: Prentice-Hall, 1983.

Canfield, J Douglas, ed. *Twentieth Century Interpretations of Sanctuary*. Englewood Cliffs, NJ: Prentice-Hall, 1982.

*Cox, Dianne L, ed. *WF's As I Lay Dying: A Critical Casebook*. NY: Garland, 1985.

*Cox, Leland H, ed. *WF: Critical Collection*. Detroit: Gale, 1982.

Fowler, Doreen & Ann J Abadie, eds. *Fifty Years of Yoknapatawpha: F and Yoknapatawpha 1979*. Jackson: U P Mississippi, 1980.

Fowler & Abadie, eds. *"A Cosmos of My Own": F and Yoknapatawpha 1980*. Jackson: U P Mississippi, 1981.

Fowler & Abadie, eds. *F: International Perspectives: F and Yoknapatawpha 1982*. Jackson: U P Mississippi, 1984.

Fowler & Abadie, eds. *New Directions in F Studies: F and Yoknapatawpha 1983*. Jackson: U P Mississippi, 1984.

Fowler & Abadie, eds. *F and Humor: F and Yoknapatawpha 1984*. Jackson: U P Mississippi, 1986.

Hoffman, Frederick J & Olga Vickery, eds. *WF: Three Decades of Criticism*. East Lansing: Michigan State U P, 1960.

*Kinney, Arthur, ed. *Critical Essays on WF: The Compson Family*. Boston: Hall, 1982.

*Kinney, ed. *Critical Essays on WF: The Sartoris Family*. Boston: Hall, 1985.

*Kinney, ed. *Critical Essays on WF: The McCaslin Family*. Boston: Hall, 1989.

Meriwether, James B, ed. *A F Miscellany*. Jackson: U P Mississippi, 1974.

Millgate, Michael, ed. *New Essays on Light in August*. Cambridge: Cambridge U P, 1987.

*Muhlenfeld, Elisabeth, ed. *WF's Absalom, Absalom!: A Critical Casebook*. NY: Garland, 1984.

*Pitavy, François L, ed. *WF's Light in August: A Critical Casebook*. NY: Garland, 1982.

Wagner, Linda Welshimer, ed. *WF: Four Decades of Criticism*. East Lansing: Michigan State U P, 1973.

*Warren, Robert Penn, ed. *F: A Collection of Critical Essays*. Englewood Cliffs, NJ: Prentice-Hall, 1966.

SPECIAL JOURNALS

The Faulkner Journal (semiannually, Fall 1985–).

The Faulkner Newsletter (quarterly, 1981–).

Faulkner Studies (semiannually, 1951–1954).

Faulkner Studies (1980).

Mississippi Quarterly (1963–). Annual Summer WF Issue.

BOOK SECTIONS

*Brodhead, Richard H. "Introduction: F and the Logic of Remaking." Brodhead, 1–19.

Brooks, Cleanth. "F's Treatment of the Racial Problem: Typical Examples." *A Shaping Joy* (NY: Harcourt Brace Jovanovich, 1971), 230–246. Rpt Cox, *WF: Critical Collection*.

Broughton, Panthea Reid. "The Cubist Novel: Toward Defining the Genre," "F's Cubist Novels." Fowler & Abadie, "*A Cosmos of My Own*," 36–58, 59–94.

Broughton. "An Amazing Gift: The Early Essays and F's Apprenticeship in Aesthetics and Criticism." Fowler & Abadie, *New Directions in F Studies*, 322–357.

Carothers, James B. "The Myriad Heart: The Evolution of the F Hero." Fowler & Abadie, "*A Cosmos of My Own*," 252–283.

*Coindreau, Maurice E. "Préface." *Le bruit et la fureur* by WF; trans Coindreau (Paris: Gallimard, 1938), 7–16. Rpt (trans George Reeves), Coindreau, *The Time of WF*.

Collins, Carvel. "The Interior Monologues of *The Sound and the Fury*." *EIE 1952* (NY: Columbia U P, 1954), 29–56.

*Cowley, Malcolm. "Introduction." *The Portable Faulkner* (NY: Viking, rev 1967), vii–xxxiii.

Davis, Walter, "The Act of Interpretation: F's 'The Bear' and the Problems of Practical Criticism." *The Act of Interpretation* (Chicago: U Chicago P, 1978), 1–61.

Dimino, Andrea. "The Dream of the Present: Time, Creativity, and the Sartoris Family." Kinney, *Critical Essays on WF: The Sartoris Family,* 332–361.

*Douglass, Paul. "Deciphering F's Uninterrupted Sentence," "F and the Bergsonian Self." *Bergson, Eliot, and American Literature* (Lexington: U Kentucky P, 1986), 118–141, 142–165.

Ellison, Ralph. "Twentieth-Century Fiction and the Black Mask of Humanity." *Shadow and Act* (NY: Random House, 1964), 24–44.

Friedman, Alan Warren. "F's Snopes Trilogy: Omniscience as Impressionism." *Multivalence: The Moral Quality of Form in the Modern Novel* (Baton Rouge: Louisiana State U P, 1978), 141–177.

Guerard, Albert J. "*Absalom, Absalom!:* The Novel as Impressionist Art." *The Triumph of the Novel: Dickens, Dostoevsky, F* (NY: Oxford U P, 1976), 302–339, 354–355.

Guetti, James. "*Absalom, Absalom!:* The Extended Simile." *The Limits of Metaphor: A Study of Melville, Conrad, and F* (Ithaca, NY: Cornell U P, 1967), 69–108. Rpt Muhlenfeld.

*Hinkle, James. "Some Yoknapatawpha Names." Fowler & Abadie, *New Directions in F Studies,* 172–201.

Kartiganer, Donald M. "Quentin Compson and F's Drama of the Generations." Kinney, *Critical Essays on WF: The Compson Family,* 381–401.

Kreiswirth, Martin. "Plots and Counterplots: The Structure of *Light in August.*" Millgate, *New Essays on Light in August,* 55–79.

Lind, Ilse Dusoir. "F's Relationship to Jews: A Beginning." Fowler & Abadie, *New Directions in F Studies,* 119–142.

Meats, Stephen. "The Chronology of *Light in August.*" Pitavy, *WF's Light in August,* 227–235.

Merton, Thomas. "'Baptism in the Forest': Wisdom and Initiation in WF." *Mansions of the Spirit,* ed George Panichas (NY: Hawthorn, 1967), 17–44.

Millgate, Michael. "WF: The Problem of Point of View." *Patterns of Commitment in American Literature,* ed Marston LaFrance (Toronto: U Toronto P, 1967), 181–192.

Millgate. "'A Cosmos of My Own': The Evolution of Yoknapatawpha." Fowler & Abadie, *Fifty Years of Yoknapatawpha,* 23–43.

Millgate. "'A Novel: Not an Anecdote': F's *Light in August.*" Millgate, *New Essays on Light in August,* 31–53.

Morrison, Gail Moore. "The Composition of *The Sound and the Fury*." Bleikasten, *WF's The Sound and the Fury*, 33–64.

Morrison. "The House That Tull Built." Cox, *WF's As I Lay Dying*, 159–177.

Patten, Catherine. "The Narrative Design of *As I Lay Dying*." Cox, *WF's As I Lay Dying*, 3–29.

Pitavy, François. "The Gothicism of *Absalom, Absalom!*: Rosa Coldfield Revisited." Fowler & Abadie, *"A Cosmos of My Own,"* 199–226.

Pitavy. "The Narrative Voice and Function of Shreve: Remarks on the Production of Meaning in *Absalom, Absalom!*" Muhlenfeld, 189–205.

Pitavy. "'Anything but Earth': The Disastrous and Necessary Sartoris Game." Kinney, *Critical Essays on WF: The Sartoris Family*, 267–273.

Polk, Noel. "'The Dungeon Was Mother Herself': WF, 1927–1931." Fowler & Abadie, *New Directions in F Studies*, 61–93.

Sundquist, Eric J. "Death, Grief, Analogous Form: *As I Lay Dying*." *Philosophical Approaches to Literature*, ed William E Cain (Lewisburg, Pa: Bucknell U P, 1983), 165–182.

Van Antwerp, Margaret A, ed. "WF." *Dictionary of Literary Biography Documentary Series*, Vol 2 (Detroit: Bruccoli Clark/Gale, 1982), 127–208.

Watkins, Evan. "The Fiction of Interpretation: F's *Absalom, Absalom!*" *The Critical Act: Criticism and Community* (New Haven, Conn: Yale U P, 1978), 188–212.

Welsh, Alexander. "On the Difference Between Prevailing and Enduring." Millgate, *New Essays on Light in August*, 123–147.

Wilder, Amos N. "F and Vestigial Moralities." *Theology and Modern Literature* (Cambridge: Harvard U P, 1958), 113–131, 139–140. Rpt as "Vestigial Moralities in *The Sound and the Fury*," Barth.

Wittenberg, Judith Bryant. "WF: A Feminist Consideration." *American Novelists Revisited: Essays in Feminist Criticism*, ed Fritz Fleischman (Boston: Hall, 1982), 325–338.

ARTICLES

Abel, Darrell. "Frozen Movement in *Light in August*." *Boston University Studies in English*, 3 (Spring 1957), 32–44. Rpt Pitavy, *WF's Light in August*.

Adamowski, T H. "Children of the Idea: Heroes and Family Romances in *Absalom, Absalom!*" *Mosaic*, 10 (Fall 1976), 115–131. Rpt Muhlenfeld.

*Adams, Richard P. "The Apprenticeship of WF." *Tulane Studies in English,* 12 (1962), 113–156. Rpt Wagner; Cox, *WF: Critical Collection.*

Adams. "Some Key Words in F." *Tulane Studies in English,* 16 (1968), 135–148.

*Aiken, Charles S. "F's Yoknapatawpha County: A Place in the American South." *Geographical Review,* 69 (Jul 1979), 331–348.

Aiken, Conrad. "WF: The Novel as Form." *Atlantic,* 164 (Nov 1939), 650–654. Rpt Hoffman & Vickery; Warren; Wagner; Bassett, *WF: The Critical Heritage.*

Arnold, Edwin T. "Freedom and Stasis in F's *Mosquitoes.*" *Mississippi Quarterly,* 28 (Summer 1975), 281–297.

Arpad, Joseph J. "WF's Legendary Novels: The Snopes Trilogy." *Mississippi Quarterly,* 22 (Summer 1969), 214–225. Rpt Cox, *WF: Critical Collection.*

Asselineau, Roger. "The French Face of WF." *Tulane Studies in English,* 23 (1978), 157–173.

*Aswell, Duncan. "The Puzzling Design of *Absalom, Absalom!*" *Kenyon Review,* 30, no 1 (1968), 67–84. Rpt Muhlenfeld.

Baldwin, James. "F and Desegregation." *Partisan Review,* 23 (Fall 1956), 568–573.

Beck, Warren. "F's Point of View." *College English,* 2 (May 1941), 736–749. Rpt Cox, *WF: Critical Collection.*

Bedient, Calvin. "Pride and Nakedness: *As I Lay Dying.*" *Modern Language Quarterly,* 29 (Mar 1968), 61–76. Rpt Cox, *WF: Critical Collection;* Cox, *WF's As I Lay Dying.*

Benson, Carl. "Thematic Design in *Light in August.*" *South Atlantic Quarterly,* 53 (Oct 1954), 540–555. Rpt Wagner; Pitavy, *WF's Light in August.*

Blanchard, Margaret. "The Rhetoric of Communion: Voice in *The Sound and the Fury.*" *American Literature,* 41 (Jan 1970), 555–565. Rpt Bleikasten, *WF's The Sound and the Fury.*

Bowling, Lawrence Edward. "F: Technique of *The Sound and the Fury.*" *Kenyon Review,* 10 (Autumn 1948), 552–566.

Bradford, M E. "A Late Encounter: F's 'Mountain Victory.'" *Mississippi Quarterly,* 40 (Fall 1987), 373–381.

*Brooks, Cleanth. "F's Vision of Good and Evil." *Massachusetts Review,* 3 (Summer 1962), 692–712. Rpt *The Hidden God* by Brooks (New Haven, Conn: Yale U P, 1963). Rpt Barth, *Religious Perspectives in F's Fiction;* Wagner; Brodhead.

Broughton, Panthea Reid. "The Economy of Desire: F's Poetics, From Eroticism to Post-Impressionism." *Faulkner Journal,* 4 (Fall 1988–Spring 1989), 159–177.

Bunselmeyer, J E. "F's Narrative Styles." *American Literature,* 53 (Nov 1981), 424–442.

Cecil, L Moffitt. "A Rhetoric for Benjy." *Southern Literary Journal,* 3 (Fall 1970), 35–46. Rpt Bleikasten, *WF's The Sound and the Fury.*

Chappel, Deborah K. "Pa Says: The Rhetoric of F's Anse Bundren." *Mississippi Quarterly,* 44 (Summer 1991), 273–285.

Chappell, Fred. "The Comic Structure of *The Sound and the Fury.*" *Mississippi Quarterly,* 31 (Summer 1978), 381–386. Rpt Bleikasten, *WF's The Sound and the Fury.*

Clarke, Deborah L. "Familiar and Fantastic: Women in *Absalom, Absalom!*" *Faulkner Journal,* 2 (Fall 1986), 62–72.

Coleman, Rosemary. "Family Ties: Generating Narratives in *Absalom, Absalom!*" *Mississippi Quarterly,* 41 (Summer 1988), 421–431.

Collins, R G. "*Light in August:* F's Stained Glass Triptych." *Mosaic,* 7 (Fall 1973), 97–157. Excerpted as "The Other Competitors for the Cross: Joanna Burden and Gail Hightower." Pitavy, *WF's Light in August.*

Cox, Dianne Luce. "A Measure of Innocence: *Sanctuary*'s Temple Drake." *Mississippi Quarterly,* 39 (Summer 1986), 301–324.

Dalziel, Pamela. "*Absalom, Absalom!:* The Extension of Dialogic Form." *Mississippi Quarterly,* 45 (Summer 1992), 277–294.

Davis, Boyd. "Caddy Compson's Eden." *Mississippi Quarterly,* 30 (Summer 1977), 381–394.

Davis, Robert Con. "The Symbolic Father in Yoknapatawpha County." *Journal of Narrative Technique,* 10 (Winter 1980), 39–55.

Degenfelder, E Pauline. "Yoknapatawpha Baroque: A Stylistic Analysis of *As I Lay Dying.*" *Style,* 7 (Spring 1973), 121–156. Rpt Cox, *WF's As I Lay Dying.*

Duvall, John N. "Murder and the Communities: Ideology in and Around *Light in August.*" *Novel,* 20 (Winter 1987), 101–122.

Duvert, Elizabeth. "F's Map of Time." *Faulkner Journal,* 2 (Fall 1986), 14–28.

Feldman, Robert L. "In Defense of Reverend Hightower: It Is Never Too Late." *College Language Association Journal,* 29 (Mar 1986), 352–367.

Ficken, Carl. "The Christ Story in *A Fable.*" *Mississippi Quarterly,* 23 (Summer 1970), 251–264.

Flint, R W. "F as Elegist." *Hudson Review,* 7 (Summer 1954), 246–257. Rpt Cox, *WF: Critical Collection.*

Garrett, George, Jr. "An Examination of the Poetry of WF." *Princeton University Library Chronicle,* 18 (Spring 1957), 124–135. Rpt Wagner.

Garrett. "F's Early Literary Criticism." *Texas Studies in Literature and Language,* 1 (Spring 1959), 3–10.

Garrison, Joseph M, Jr. "Perception, Language, and Reality in *As I Lay Dying.*" *Arizona Quarterly,* 32 (Spring 1976), 16–30. Rpt Cox, *WF's As I Lay Dying.*

Gidley, Mick. "One Continuous Force: Notes on F's Extra-Literary Reading." *Mississippi Quarterly,* 23 (Summer 1970), 299–314. Rpt Wagner.

Gold, Joseph. "The 'Normality' of Snopesism: Universal Themes in F's *The Hamlet.*" *Wisconsin Studies in Contemporary Literature,* 3 (Winter 1962), 25–34. Rpt Wagner; Cox, *WF: Critical Collection.*

Gordon, Caroline. "Notes on F and Flaubert." *Hudson Review,* 1 (Summer 1948), 222–231. Rpt *The House of Fiction* by Gordon & Allen Tate (NY: Scribners, 1950).

Greet, T Y. "The Theme and Structure of F's *The Hamlet.*" *PMLA,* 72 (Sep 1957), 775–790. Rpt Hoffman & Vickery; Wagner.

Gross, Beverly. "Form and Fulfillment in *The Sound and the Fury.*" *Modern Language Quarterly,* 29 (Dec 1968), 439–449. Rpt Bleikasten, *WF's The Sound and the Fury.*

Hagopian, John V. "Nihilism in F's *The Sound and the Fury.*" *Modern Fiction Studies,* 13 (Spring 1967), 45–55.

*Hagopian. "The Biblical Background of F's *Absalom, Absalom!*" *CEA Critic,* 36 (Jan 1973), 1, 22–24. Rpt Muhlenfeld.

Hayhoe, George F. "WF's *Flags in the Dust.*" *Mississippi Quarterly,* 28 (Summer 1975), 370–386.

Heller, Terry. "Mirrored Worlds and the Gothic in F's *Sanctuary.*" *Mississippi Quarterly,* 42 (Summer 1989), 247–259.

Hunt, John W. "Keeping the Hoop Skirts Out: Historiography in F's *Absalom, Absalom!*" *Faulkner Studies,* 1 (1980), 38–47.

Johnson, Julie M. "The Theory of Relativity in Modern Literature: An Overview and *The Sound and the Fury.*" *Journal of Modern Literature,* 10 (Jun 1983), 217–230.

Justus, James H. "The Epic Design of *Absalom, Absalom!*" *Texas Studies in Literature and Language,* 4 (Summer 1962), 157–176. Rpt Muhlenfeld.

*Kartiganer, Donald M. "The Farm and the Journey: Ways of Mourning and Meaning in *As I Lay Dying.*" *Mississippi Quarterly,* 43 (Summer 1990), 281–303.

*Kidd, Millie M. "The Dialogic Perspective in WF's *The Hamlet.*" *Mississippi Quarterly,* 44 (Summer 1991), 309–320.

Kinney, Arthur F. "F and Flaubert." *Journal of Modern Literature,* 6 (Apr 1977), 222–247.

Korenman, Joan S. "F's Grecian Urn." *Southern Literary Journal,* 7 (Fall 1974), 3–23. Excerpted Pitavy, *WF's Light in August.*

Krause, David. "Reading Bon's Letter and F's *Absalom, Absalom!*" *PMLA,* 99 (Mar 1984), 225–241.

Leahy, Sharon L. "Poker and Semantics: Unravelling the Gordian Knot in F's 'Was.'" *American Literature,* 57 (Mar 1985), 129–137.

Lilly, Paul R, Jr. "Caddy and Addie: Speakers of F's Impeccable Language." *Journal of Narrative Technique,* 3 (Sep 1973), 170–182.

Lind, Ilse Dusoir. "The Design and Meaning of *Absalom, Absalom!*" *PMLA,* 70 (Dec 1955), 887–912. Rpt Hoffman & Vickery; Wagner.

Martin, Timothy P. "The Art and Rhetoric of Chronology in F's *Light in August.*" *College Literature,* 7 (Spring 1980), 125–135.

Mathews, Laura. "Shaping the Life of Man: Darl Bundren as Supplementary Narrator in *As I Lay Dying.*" *Journal of Narrative Technique,* 16 (Fall 1986), 231–245.

Matlack, James H. "The Voices of Time: Narrative Structure in *Absalom, Absalom!*" *Southern Review,* 15 (Apr 1979), 333–354.

Matthews, John T. "The Elliptical Nature of *Sanctuary.*" *Novel,* 17 (Spring 1984), 246–265.

McHaney, Thomas L. "*Sanctuary* and Frazer's Slain Kings." *Mississippi Quarterly,* 24 (Summer 1971), 223–245. Rpt Canfield.

McHaney. "The Elmer Papers: F's Comic Portraits of the Artist." *Mississippi Quarterly,* 26 (Summer 1973), 281–311. Rpt Meriwether, *F Miscellany.*

Meriwether, James B. "Blotner's F." *Mississippi Quarterly,* 28 (Summer 1975), 353–369.

Millgate, Michael. "F on the Literature of the First World War." *Mississippi Quarterly,* 26 (Summer 1973), 387–393. Rpt Meriwether, *F Miscellany.*

Millgate. "Starting Out in the Twenties: Reflections on *Soldiers' Pay.*" *Mosaic,* 7 (Fall 1973), 1–14. Rpt Cox, *WF: Critical Collection.*

*Millgate. "F's Masters." *Tulane Studies in English,* 23 (1978), 143–155. Rpt Cox, *WF: Critical Collection.*

Morrison, Gail Moore. "'Time, Tide, and Twilight': *Mayday* and F's Quest Toward *The Sound and the Fury.*" *Mississippi Quarterly,* 31 (Summer 1978), 337–357.

Mortimer, Gail L. "The Ironies of Transcendent Love in F's *The Wild Palms.*" *Faulkner Journal,* 1 (Spring 1986), 30–42.

*Muhlenfeld, Elisabeth. "Shadows With Substance and Ghosts Exhumed: The Women in *Absalom, Absalom!*" *Mississippi Quarterly,* 25 (Summer 1972), 289–304.

Muhlenfeld. "'We Have Waited Long Enough': Judith Sutpen and Charles Bon." *Southern Review,* 14 (Jan 1978), 66–80. Rpt Muhlenfeld.

Nicolaisen, Peter. "'The dark land talking the voiceless speech': F and 'Native Soil.'" *Mississippi Quarterly,* 45 (Summer 1992), 253–276.

O'Donnell, George Marion. "F's Mythology." *Kenyon Review,* 1 (Summer 1939), 285–299. Rpt Hoffman & Vickery; Warren; Wagner.

Palliser, Charles. "Fate and Madness: The Determinist Vision of Darl Bundren." *American Literature,* 49 (Jan 1978), 619–633. Rpt Cox, *WF's As I Lay Dying.*

Parr, Susan Resneck. "The Fourteenth Image of the Blackbird: Another Look at Truth in *Absalom, Absalom!*" *Arizona Quarterly,* 35 (Summer 1979), 153–164.

Phillips, K J. "F in the Garden of Eden." *Southern Humanities Review,* 19 (Winter 1985), 1–19.

Pladott, Dinnah. "F's *A Fable:* A Heresy of a Declaration of Faith." *Journal of Narrative Technique,* 12 (Spring 1982), 73–94.

Polk, Noel. "WF's *Marionettes.*" *Mississippi Quarterly,* 26 (Summer 1973), 247–280. Rpt Meriwether, *F Miscellany.*

Prior, Linda T. "Theme, Imagery, and Structure in *The Hamlet.*" *Mississippi Quarterly,* 22 (Summer 1969), 237–256.

Radloff, Bernhard. "The Unity of Time in *The Sound and the Fury.*" *Faulkner Journal,* 1 (Spring 1986), 56–68.

Rio-Jelliffe, R. "*Absalom, Absalom!* as Self-Reflexive Novel." *Journal of Narrative Technique,* 11 (Spring 1981), 75–90.

Rooks, George. "Vardaman's Journey in *As I Lay Dying.*" *Arizona Quarterly,* 35 (Summer 1979), 114–128. Rpt Cox, *WF's As I Lay Dying.*

Ross, Stephen M. "Rev. Shegog's Powerful Voice." *Faulkner Journal,* 1 (Fall 1985), 8–16.

Rossky, William. "*As I Lay Dying:* The Insane World." *Texas Studies in Literature and Language,* 4 (Spring 1962), 87–95. Rpt Cox, *WF's As I Lay Dying.*

Rossky. "The Pattern of Nightmare in *Sanctuary;* or, Miss Reba's Dogs." *Modern Fiction Studies,* 15 (Winter 1969–1970), 503–515. Rpt Canfield.

Sartre, Jean-Paul. "A propos de 'Le Bruit et la Fureur': La temporalité chez F." *Nouvelle Revue Française,* 52 (Jun 1939), 1057–1061; 53 (Jul 1939), 147–151. Rpt (trans) Hoffman & Vickery; Warren.

Scott, Arthur L. "The Myriad Perspectives of *Absalom, Absalom!*" *American Quarterly,* 6 (Fall 1954), 210–220. Rpt Muhlenfeld.

Singleton, Marvin K. "Personae at Law and in Equity: The Unity of F's *Absalom, Absalom!*" *Papers on Language and Literature,* 3 (Fall 1967), 354–370.

Slabey, Robert M. "Myth and Ritual in *Light in August.*" *Texas Studies in Literature and Language,* 2 (Autumn 1960), 328–349.

Smith, Meredith. "A Chronology of *Go Down, Moses.*" *Mississippi Quarterly,* 36 (Summer 1983), 319–328.

St Clair, Janet. "The Necessity of Signifying Something: Quentin Compson's Rejection of Despair." *Mississippi Quarterly,* 43 (Summer 1990), 317–334.

Taylor, Carole Anne. "*Light in August:* The Epistemology of Tragic Paradox." *Texas Studies in Literature and Language,* 22 (Spring 1980), 48–68. Rpt Pitavy, *WF's Light in August.*

Thornton, Weldon. "Structure and Theme in F's *Go Down, Moses.*" *Costerus,* ns 3 (1975), 73–112. Rpt Cox, *WF: Critical Collection.*

Toles, George. "The Space Between: A Study of F's *Sanctuary.*" *Texas Studies in Literature and Language,* 22 (Spring 1980), 22–47. Rpt Canfield.

Tucker, John. "WF's *As I Lay Dying*: Working Out the Cubistic Bugs." *Texas Studies in Literature and Language,* 26 (Winter 1984), 388–404.

Wall, Carey. "Drama and Technique in F's *The Hamlet.*" *Twentieth Century Literature,* 14 (Apr 1968), 17–23.

Warren, Marsha. "Time, Space and Semiotic Discourse in the Feminization/Disintegration of Quentin Compson." *Faulkner Journal,* 4 (Fall 1988–Spring 1989), 99–111.

Warren, Robert Penn. "Not Local Color." *Virginia Quarterly Review,* 8 (Jan 1932), 153–160.

*Warren. "The Snopes World." *Kenyon Review,* 3 (Spring 1941), 253–257. Rpt Bassett, *WF: The Critical Heritage.*

*Warren. "Cowley's F." *New Republic,* 115 (12 Aug 1946), 176–180; 115 (26 Aug 1946), 234–237. Rpt Bassett, *WF: The Critical Heritage.*

Watkins, Floyd C. "What Happens in *Absalom, Absalom!*" *Modern Fiction Studies,* 13 (Spring 1967), 79–87. Rpt Muhlenfeld.

*Watson, James G. "Carvel Collins's Faulkner: A Newly Opened Archive." *Library Chronicle of the University of Texas,* 20, no 4 (1991), 17–35. Rpt *Mississippi Quarterly,* 44 (Summer 1991), 257–272.

Weinstein, Arnold. "Fusion and Confusion in *Light in August.*" *Faulkner Journal,* 1 (Spring 1986), 2–16.

Welty, Eudora. "Department of Amplification." *New Yorker,* 24 (1 Jan 1949), 50–51.

Welty. "In Yoknapatawpha." *Hudson Review,* 1 (Winter 1949), 596–598. Rpt as "WF's *Intruder in the Dust.*" *The Eye of the Story* by Welty (NY: Random House, 1978).

*Werner, Craig. "Tell Old Pharaoh: The Afro-American Response to F." *Southern Review,* 19 (Autumn 1983), 711–735.

Wilson, Edmund. "WF's Reply to the Civil-Rights Program." *New Yorker,* 24 (23 Oct 1948), 120–122, 125–128. Rpt *Classics and Commercials* by Wilson (NY: Farrar, Straus, 1950). Rpt Warren.

Wittenberg, Judith Bryant. "F and Eugene O'Neill." *Mississippi Quarterly,* 33 (Summer 1980), 327–341.

Yonce, Margaret. "'Shot Down Last Spring': The Wounded Aviators of F's Wasteland." *Mississippi Quarterly,* 31 (Summer 1978), 359–368.

Yonce. "The Composition of *Soldiers' Pay.*" *Mississippi Quarterly,* 33 (Summer 1980), 291–326.

Zink, Karl E. "WF: Form as Experience." *South Atlantic Quarterly,* 53 (Jul 1954), 384–403.

Zink. "Flux and the Frozen Moment: The Imagery of Stasis in F's Prose." *PMLA,* 71 (Jun 1956), 285–301.

Zoellner, Robert H. "F's Prose Style in *Absalom, Absalom!*" *American Literature,* 30 (Jan 1959), 486–502.

— *Thomas L. McHaney*

F. SCOTT FITZGERALD

St Paul, Minn, 24 Sep 1896–Los Angeles, Calif, 21 Dec 1940

F. Scott Fitzgerald's high critical reputation was a posthumous development. Once regarded as primarily a social chronicler, Fitzgerald has come to be perceived as a moralist. Although *This Side of Paradise* made him famous at twenty-three, during his lifetime he was more widely known as the writer of some 160 commercial short stories than as a novelist. There were reassessments of Fitzgerald's career following his death; but the Fitzgerald revival was not firmly established until the 1950s, largely in response to the romantic and tragic aspects of his life. During the first phase of this revival Fitzgerald was viewed as "the laureate of the Jazz Age" and identified with the ebullience of the 1920s. Subsequent scholarship has examined Fitzgerald's narrative technique and stylistic control, his complex treatment of the theme of aspiration in terms of character, and his sense of American history.

Bibliographies

American Literary Scholarship: An Annual, 1963– . Durham, NC: Duke U P, 1965– . Chapters on FSF.

*Bruccoli, Matthew J. *FSF: A Descriptive Bibliography: Revised Edition.* Pittsburgh, Pa: U Pittsburgh P, 1987. Primary.

*Bryer, Jackson R. *The Critical Reputation of FSF.* Hamden, Conn: Archon, 1967. *Supplement One*, 1984. Secondary.

Stanley, Linda C. *The Foreign Critical Reputation of FSF.* Westport, Conn: Greenwood, 1980.

Books

This Side of Paradise. NY: Scribners, 1920. Novel.

Flappers and Philosophers. NY: Scribners, 1920. Stories.

The Beautiful and Damned. NY: Scribners, 1922. Novel.

Tales of the Jazz Age. NY: Scribners, 1922. Stories.

The Vegetable; or, From President to Postman. NY: Scribners, 1923. Play.

The Great Gatsby. NY: Scribners, 1925. *The Great Gatsby: A Facsimile of the Manuscript*, ed with intro by Matthew J Bruccoli. Washington: Bruccoli Clark/Microcard Editions,1973. Novel.

All the Sad Young Men. NY: Scribners, 1926. Stories.

Tender Is the Night. NY: Scribners, 1934. Repub "With the Author's Final Revisions," ed Malcolm Cowley, 1951. Novel.

Taps at Reveille. NY: Scribners, 1935. Stories.

The Last Tycoon, ed with intro by Edmund Wilson. NY: Scribners, 1941. Novel.

The Crack-Up, ed with intro by Wilson. NY: New Directions, 1945. Essays & notebooks.

Afternoon of an Author, ed with intro by Arthur Mizener. Princeton, NJ: Princeton U Library, 1957. Stories & essays.

The Pat Hobby Stories, ed with intro by Arnold Gingrich. NY: Scribners, 1962.

The Apprentice Fiction of FSF, 1909–1917, ed with intro by John Kuehl. New Brunswick, NJ: Rutgers U P, 1965.

The Basil and Josephine Stories, ed with intro by Jackson R Bryer & Kuehl. NY: Scribners, 1973.

Bits of Paradise, ed with intro by Scottie Fitzgerald Smith & Bruccoli. London: Bodley Head, 1973; NY: Scribners, 1974. Stories.

FSF's Preface to This Side of Paradise, ed John R Hopkins. Iowa City, Iowa: Windhover/Bruccoli Clark, 1975.

The Cruise of the Rolling Junk, intro by Bruccoli. Bloomfield Hills, Mich & Columbia, SC: Bruccoli Clark, 1976. Essay.

FSF's Screenplay for Three Comrades, ed with afterword by Bruccoli. Carbondale & Edwardsville: Southern Illinois U P / London & Amsterdam: Feffer & Simons, 1978.

FSF's St. Paul Plays, 1911–1914, ed with intro by Alan Margolies. Princeton, NJ: Princeton U Library, 1978.

The Price Was High, ed with intro by Bruccoli. NY & London: Harcourt Brace Jovanovich/Bruccoli Clark, 1979. Stories.

Poems 1911–1940, ed Bruccoli; intro by James Dickey. Bloomfield Hills, Mich & Columbia, SC: Bruccoli Clark, 1981.

FSF Manuscripts, 18 vols, ed Bruccoli. NY & London: Garland, 1990–1991. Facsimiles.

Letters, Diaries, Notebooks

The Letters of FSF, ed with intro by Andrew Turnbull. NY: Scribners, 1963.

Thoughtbook of Francis Scott Key Fitzgerald, intro by John Kuehl. Princeton, NJ: Princeton U Library, 1965.

Dear Scott/Dear Max: The F–Perkins Correspondence, ed with intro by Kuehl & Jackson R Bryer. NY: Scribners, 1971.

As Ever, Scott Fitz—: Letters Between FSF and His Literary Agent, Harold Ober, 1919–1940, ed with intro by Matthew J Bruccoli & Jennifer Atkinson. Philadelphia & NY: Lippincott, 1972.

FSF's Ledger: A Facsimile, intro by Bruccoli. Washington: Bruccoli Clark/Microcard Editions, 1973.

The Notebooks of FSF, ed with intro by Bruccoli. NY & London: Harcourt Brace Jovanovich/Bruccoli Clark, 1978.

Correspondence of FSF, ed with intro by Bruccoli, Margaret M Duggan & Susan Walker. NY: Random House, 1980.

Other

Fie! Fie! Fi-Fi! Cincinnati, Ohio: Church, 1914. Libretto with lyrics by FSF.

The Evil Eye. Cincinnati, Ohio: Church, 1915. Libretto with lyrics by FSF.

Safety First. Cincinnati, Ohio: Church, 1916. Libretto with lyrics by FSF.

FSF: Inscriptions, ed with intro by Matthew J Bruccoli. Columbia, SC: Bruccoli, 1988.

Editions & Collections

The Portable FSF, ed Dorothy Parker; intro by John O'Hara. NY: Viking, 1945.

The Stories of FSF, ed with intro by Malcolm Cowley. NY: Scribners, 1951.

The Bodley Head SF, 6 vols. London: Bodley Head, 1958–1963.

The Stories of FSF, 5 vols. Harmondsworth, UK: Penguin, 1962–1968.

FSF in His Own Time: A Miscellany, ed with intro by Matthew J Bruccoli & Jackson R Bryer. Kent, Ohio: Kent State U P, 1971. Primary & secondary material, including interviews.

The Short Stories of FSF: A New Collection, ed with preface by Bruccoli. NY: Scribners, 1989.

The Great Gatsby, ed with intro by Bruccoli. Cambridge & c: Cambridge U P, 1991 (First vol of "The Cambridge Edition of the Works of FSF").

The Love of The Last Tycoon: A Western, ed with intro by Bruccoli. Cambridge & c: Cambridge U P, 1993 (Second vol of "The Cambridge Edition of the Works of FSF").

Manuscripts & Archives

Princeton U Library.

Concordance

Crosland, Andrew T. *A Concordance to FSF's The Great Gatsby*. Detroit: Bruccoli Clark/Gale, 1975.

Biographies

BOOKS

Bruccoli, Matthew J. *Scott and Ernest*. NY: Random House, 1978.

*Bruccoli. *Some Sort of Epic Grandeur*. San Diego: Harcourt Brace Jovanovich, 1981. Rev ed, NY: Carroll & Graf, 1992.

Buttitta, Tony. *After the Good Gay Times*. NY: Viking, 1974. Repub as *The Lost Summer*. NY: St Martin, 1987.

Donaldson, Scott. *Fool for Love*. NY: Congdon & Weed, 1983.

Graham, Sheilah & Gerold Frank. *Beloved Infidel*. NY: Holt, 1958.

*Graham. *College of One*. NY: Viking, 1967.

Graham. *The Real FSF: Thirty-five Years Later*. NY: Grossett & Dunlap, 1976.

Koblas, John J. *FSF in Minnesota*. St Paul: Minnesota Historical Society, 1978.

Latham, Aaron. *Crazy Sundays: FSF in Hollywood*. NY: Viking, 1971.

LeVot, André. *FSF*. Garden City, NY: Doubleday, 1983.

Mayfield, Sara. *Exiles From Paradise*. NY: Delacorte, 1971.

Mellow, James R. *Invented Lives*. Boston: Houghton Mifflin, 1984.

Milford, Nancy. *Zelda*. NY: Harper & Row, 1970.

Mizener, Arthur. *The Far Side of Paradise*. Boston: Houghton Mifflin, rev 1965.

Mizener. *SF and His World*. NY: Putnam, 1972.

Ring, Frances Kroll. *Against the Current: As I Remember FSF*. San Francisco: Ellis/Creative Arts, 1985.

*Smith, Scottie Fitzgerald, Bruccoli & Joan P Kerr. *The Romantic Egoists*, intro by Smith. NY: Scribners, 1974. Pictorial biography.

Turnbull, Andrew. *SF*. NY: Scribners, 1962.

BOOK SECTIONS

Berg, A Scott. *Max Perkins* (NY: Dutton, 1978), passim.

Callaghan, Morley. *That Summer in Paris* (NY: Coward-McCann, 1963), passim.

Dardis, Tom. "FSF: What Do You Do When There's Nothing to Do?" *Some Time in the Sun* (NY: Scribners, 1976), 17–78.

Dardis. "Fitzgerald." *The Thirsty Muse: Alcohol and the American Writer* (NY: Ticknor & Fields, 1989), 97–154.

Donnelly, Honoria M. *Sara and Gerald* (NY: Times, 1982), passim.

Hemingway, Ernest. "SF," "Hawks Do Not Share," "A Matter of Measurements." *A Moveable Feast* (NY: Scribners, 1964), 147–193. "SF" rpt Claridge.

Lanahan, Frances Fitzgerald. Introduction. *Six Tales of the Jazz Age and Other Stories* by FSF (NY: Scribners, 1960), 5–11.

ARTICLES

Donaldson, Scott. "FSF, Princeton '17." *Princeton University Library Chronicle*, 40 (Winter 1979), 119–154.

Fitzgerald, Frances Scott. "Princeton and FSF." *Nassau Literary Magazine,* 100 (1942), 45.

Gingrich, Arnold. "Publisher's Page—Will the Real SF Please Stand Up and Be Counted?" *Esquire,* 62 (Dec 1964), 8, 10, 12, 16.

Gingrich. "Scott, Ernest and Whoever." *Esquire,* 66 (Dec 1966), 186–189, 322–325.

Hearne, Laura Guthrie. "A Summer With FSF." *Esquire,* 62 (Dec 1964), 160–165, 232, 236–237, 240, 242, 246, 250, 252, 254–258, 260.

Schulberg, Budd. "Old Scott: The Mask, the Myth, and the Man." *Esquire,* 55 (Jan 1961), 97–101. Rpt *The Four Seasons of Success* by Schulberg (Garden City, NY: Doubleday, 1972). Rpt Claridge.

Critical Studies

BOOKS

Allen, Joan M. *Candles and Carnival Lights: The Catholic Sensibility of FSF.* NY: NYU P, 1978.

Bruccoli, Matthew J. *The Composition of Tender Is the Night.* Pittsburgh: U Pittsburgh P, 1963.

Bruccoli. *"The Last of the Novelists": FSF and The Last Tycoon.* Carbondale: Southern Illinois U P, 1977.

Callahan, John F. *The Illusions of a Nation.* Urbana: U Illinois P, 1972.

Chambers, John B. *The Novels of FSF.* NY: St Martin, 1989.

Cross, K G W. *SF.* NY: Grove, 1964.

Dixon, Wheeler W. *The Cinematic Vision of FSF.* Ann Arbor, Mich: UMI, 1986.

*Eble, Kenneth. *FSF.* NY: Twayne, rev 1977.

Fahey, William A. *FSF and the American Dream.* NY: Crowell, 1973.

Fryer, Sarah Beebe. *F's New Women: Harbingers of Change.* Ann Arbor, Mich: UMI, 1988.

Goldhurst, William. *FSF and His Contemporaries.* Cleveland, Ohio: World, 1963.

Higgins, John A. *FSF: A Study of the Stories.* NY: St John's U P, 1971.

Hook, Andrew. *FSF.* London: Arnold, 1992.

Lehan, Richard D. *FSF and the Craft of Fiction.* Carbondale: Southern Illinois U P, 1966.

Lehan. *The Great Gatsby: The Limits of Wonder.* Boston: Twayne: 1990.

Long, Robert Emmet. *The Achieving of The Great Gatsby.* Lewisburg, Pa: Bucknell U P, 1979.

Lowry, Malcolm & Margerie. *Notes on a Screenplay for FSF's Tender Is the Night.* Bloomfield Hills, Mich: Bruccoli Clark, 1976.

Mangum, Bryant. *A Fortune Yet: Money in the Art of FSF's Short Stories.* NY: Garland, 1991.

Matterson, Stephen. *The Great Gatsby.* London: Macmillan, 1990.

Miller, James E, Jr. *FSF: His Art and His Technique*. NY: NYU P, 1964.

Parkinson, Kathleen. *FSF: Tender Is the Night*. Harmondsworth, UK: Penguin, 1986.

Parkinson. *FSF: The Great Gatsby*. Harmondsworth, UK: Penguin, 1987.

Perosa, Sergio. *The Art of FSF*. Ann Arbor: U Michigan P, 1965.

Piper, Henry Dan. *FSF: A Critical Portrait*. NY: Holt, Rinehart & Winston, 1965.

Seiters, Dan. *Image Patterns in the Novels of FSF*. Ann Arbor, Mich: UMI, 1986.

Shain, Charles E. *FSF*. Minneapolis: U Minnesota P, 1961.

*Sklar, Robert. *FSF: The Last Laocoön*. NY: Oxford U P, 1967.

Stavola, Thomas J. *SF: Crisis in an American Identity*. NY: Barnes & Noble, 1979.

Way, Brian. *FSF and the Art of Social Fiction*. NY: St Martin, 1980.

Whitley, John S. *FSF: The Great Gatsby*. London: Arnold, 1976.

COLLECTIONS OF ESSAYS

Bloom, Harold, ed. *FSF*. NY: Chelsea House, 1985.

Bloom, ed. *FSF's The Great Gatsby*. NY: Chelsea House, 1986.

Bloom, ed. *Gatsby*. NY: Chelsea House, 1991.

Bruccoli, Matthew J, ed. *Profile of FSF*. Columbus, Ohio: Merrill, 1971.

*Bruccoli, ed. *New Essays on The Great Gatsby*. Cambridge: Cambridge U P, 1985.

*Bryer, Jackson R, ed. *FSF: The Critical Reception*. NY: Franklin, 1978.

*Bryer, ed. *The Short Stories of FSF*. Madison: U Wisconsin P, 1982.

*Claridge, Henry, ed. *FSF: Critical Assessments*, 4 vols. Mountfield, UK: Helm, 1991.

Cowley, Malcolm & Robert, eds. *F and the Jazz Age*. NY: Scribners, 1966.

*Donaldson, Scott, ed. *Critical Essays on FSF's The Great Gatsby*. Boston: Hall, 1984.

Eble, Kenneth, ed. *FSF: A Collection of Criticism*. NY: McGraw-Hill, 1973.

*Hoffman, Frederick J, ed. *The Great Gatsby: A Study*. NY: Scribners, 1962.

Kazin, Alfred, ed. *FSF: The Man and His Work*. Cleveland, Ohio: World, 1951.

LaHood, Marvin J, ed. *Tender Is the Night: Essays in Criticism*. Bloomington: Indiana U P, 1969.

Lee, A Robert, ed. *SF: The Promises of Life*. London: Vision / NY: St Martin, 1989.

Lockridge, Ernest, ed. *Twentieth Century Interpretations of The Great Gatsby*. Englewood Cliffs, NJ: Prentice-Hall, 1968.

Mizener, Arthur, ed. *FSF: A Collection of Critical Essays*. Englewood Cliffs, NJ: Prentice-Hall, 1963.

*Piper, Henry Dan, ed. *F's The Great Gatsby*. NY: Scribners, 1970.

*Stern, Milton R, ed. *Critical Essays on FSF's Tender Is the Night*. Boston: Hall, 1986.

University of Minnesota Conference on FSF. . . Proceedings. Minneapolis: U Minnesota, 1982.

Wilson, Edmund, ed. *The Crack-Up*, 308–347.

SPECIAL JOURNALS

Fitzgerald/Hemingway Annual (1969–1979). Washington: Microcard Editions, 1969–1976; Detroit: Bruccoli Clark/Gale, 1977–1979. Includes checklists.

Fitzgerald Newsletter (quarterly, 1958–1968). Washington: Microcard Editions, 1969. Includes checklists.

Modern Fiction Studies, 7 (Spring 1961). FSF issue.

BOOK SECTIONS

Buell, Lawrence. "The Significance of Fantasy in F's Short Fiction." Bryer (1982), 23–38. Rpt Claridge.

Carrithers, Gale H. "F's Triumph." Hoffman, 303–320.

Doherty, William E. "*Tender Is the Night* and the 'Ode to a Nightingale.'" *Explorations of Literature*, ed Rima D Reck (Baton Rouge: Louisiana State U P, 1966), 100–114. Rpt Lahood, Eble, Bloom (1985), Stern, Claridge.

Donaldson, Scott. "Money and Marriage in F's Stories." Bryer (1982), 75–88. Rpt Claridge.

Eble, Kenneth. "Touches of Disaster: Alcoholism and Mental Illness in F's Short Stories." Bryer (1982), 39–52.

*Garrett, George. "Fire and Freshness: A Matter of Style in *The Great Gasby*." Bruccoli (1985), 101–116.

Kenner, Hugh. "The Promised Land." *A Homemade World* (NY: Knopf, 1975), 20–49. Rpt Bloom (1991), Claridge.

Langman, F H. "Style and Shape in *The Great Gatsby.*" Donaldson, 31–53.

Lehan, Richard D. "The Romantic Self and the Uses of Place in the Stories of FSF." Bryer (1982), 3–22.

Miller, James E. "F's *Gatsby:* The World as Ash Heap." Donaldson, 242–259.

O'Hara, John. "On FSF." *"An Artist Is His Own Fault:" John O'Hara on Writers and Writing,* ed Matthew J Bruccoli (Carbondale: Southern Illinois U P, 1977), 135–154.

*Trilling, Lionel. "FSF." *The Liberal Imagination* (NY: Viking, 1950), 243–254. Rpt Hoffman, Mizener, Donaldson, Bloom (1985), Claridge.

*Van Antwerp, Margaret A, ed. "FSF." *Dictionary of Literary Biography Documentary Series,* Vol 1 (Detroit: Bruccoli Clark/Gale, 1982), 239–290.

ARTICLES

Atkinson, Jennifer. "The Lost and Unpublished Stories of FSF." *Fitzgerald/Hemingway Annual* (1971), 32–63.

Berryman, John. "FSF." *Kenyon Review,* 8 (Winter 1946), 103–112. Rpt Claridge.

*Bewley, Marius. "SF's Criticism of America." *Sewanee Review,* 62 (Spring 1954), 223–246. Rpt Hoffman, Mizener, Lockridge. Augmented as "SF and the Collapse of the American Dream." *The Eccentric Design* by Bewley (NY: Columbia U P, 1959). Rpt Bloom (1985), Claridge.

Bicknell, John W. "The Waste Land of FSF." *Virginia Quarterly Review,* 30 (Autumn 1954), 556–572. Rpt Eble, Claridge.

Bishop, John Peale. "The Missing All." *Virginia Quarterly Review,* 13 (Winter 1937), 106–121.

Bryer, Jackson R. "Four Decades of F Studies: The Best and the Brightest." *Twentieth Century Literature,* 26 (Summer 1980), 247–267.

Corso, Joseph. "One Not-Forgotten Summer Night: Sources for Fictional Symbols of American Character in *The Great Gatsby.*" *Fitzgerald/Hemingway Annual* (1976), 9–34.

Cowley, Malcolm. "Third Act and Epilogue." *New Yorker,* 21 (30 Jun 1945), 53–54, 57–58. Rpt Kazin, Mizener.

Cowley. "The SF Story." *New Republic,* 124 (12 Feb 1951), 17–20.

Cowley. "F: The Double Man." *Saturday Review of Literature,* 34 (24 Feb 1951), 9–10, 42–44.

*Cowley. "FSF: The Romance of Money." *Western Review,* 17 (Summer 1953), 245–255. Rpt Piper.

Donaldson, Scott. "SF's Romance With the South." *Southern Literary Journal,* 5 (Spring 1973), 3–17.

Donaldson. "The Crisis of F's 'Crack-Up.'" *Twentieth Century Literature,* 26 (Summer 1980), 171-188. Rpt Claridge.

Donaldson. "The Political Development of FSF." *Prospects,* 6 (1981), 313–355.

Dos Passos, John. "F and the Press." *New Republic,* 104 (17 Feb 1941), 213. Rpt Wilson, Kazin, Claridge.

Doyno, Victor A. "Patterns in *The Great Gatsby.*" *Modern Fiction Studies,* 12 (Winter 1966–1967), 415–426. Rpt Piper.

Eble, Kenneth. "The Craft of Revision: *The Great Gatsby.*" *American Literature,* 36 (Autumn 1964), 315–326. Rpt Piper, Donaldson.

Friedrich, Otto. "Reappraisals—FSF: Money, Money, Money." *American Scholar,* 29 (Summer 1960), 392–405. Rpt Claridge.

Fussell, Edwin S. "F's Brave New World." *ELH,* 19 (Dec 1952), 291–306. Rpt Hoffman, Mizener, Stern, Claridge.

Gervais, Ronald J. "The Socialist and the Silk Stockings: F's Double Allegiance." *Mosaic,* 15 (Jun 1982), 79–92. Rpt Bloom (1985).

*Goodwin, Donald W. "The Alcoholism of F." *Journal of the American Medical Association,* 212 (6 Apr 1970), 86–90.

Hanzo, Thomas A. "The Theme and the Narrator of *The Great Gatsby.*" *Modern Fiction Studies,* 2 (Winter 1956–1957), 183–190. Rpt Hoffman, Lockridge.

Harding, D W. "SF." *Scrutiny,* 18 (Winter 1951–1952), 166–174. Rpt Claridge.

Harvey, W J. "Theme and Texture in *The Great Gatsby.*" *English Studies,* 38, no 1 (1957), 12–20. Rpt Lockridge, Donaldson, Claridge.

*Haywood, Lynn. "Historical Notes for *This Side of Paradise.*" *Resources for American Literary Study,* 10 (Autumn 1980), 191–208.

*Kuehl, John. "SF: Romantic and Realist." *Texas Studies in Literature and Language,* 1 (Autumn 1959), 412–426.

*Kuehl. "SF's Reading." *Princeton University Library Chronicle,* 22 (Winter 1961), 58–89. Rpt Bruccoli (1971).

*Kuehl. "SF's Critical Opinions." *Modern Fiction Studies,* 7 (Spring 1961), 3–18. Rpt Bruccoli (1971), Claridge.

Larsen, Erling. "The Geography of F's Saint Paul." *Carleton Miscellany,* 13 (Spring–Summer 1973), 3–30.

Lehan, Richard D. "FSF and Romantic Destiny." *Twentieth Century Literature*, 26 (Summer 1980), 137–156.

LeVot, André. "F in Paris." *Fitzgerald/Hemingway Annual* (1973), 49–68.

*MacKendrick, Paul L. "The Great Gatsby and Trimalchio." *Classical Journal*, 45 (Apr 1950), 307–314.

Mann, Charles. "FSF's Critique of *A Farewell to Arms.*" *Fitzgerald/Hemingway Annual* (1976), 140–153.

Margolies, Alan. "F's Work in the Film Studios." *Princeton University Library Chronicle*, 32 (Winter 1971), 81–110.

Moyer, Kermit W. "*The Great Gatsby*: F's Meditation on American History." *Fitzgerald/Hemingway Annual* (1972), 43–58. Rpt Donaldson.

Ornstein, Robert. "SF's Fable of East and West." *College English*, 18 (Dec 1956), 139–143. Rpt Lockridge, Eble, Bloom (1985), Claridge.

Prigozy, Ruth. "Poor Butterfly: FSF and Popular Music." *Prospects*, 2 (1976), 41–67.

Raleigh, John Henry. "FSF's *The Great Gatsby*: Legendary Bases and Allegorical Significances." *University of Kansas City Review*, 24 (Autumn 1957), 55–58. Rpt Mizener, Piper.

Samuels, Charles T. "The Greatness of 'Gatsby.'" *Massachusetts Review*, 7 (Autumn 1966), 783–794. Rpt Piper.

Savage, D S. "The Significance of FSF." *Arizona Quarterly*, 8 (Autumn 1952), 197–210. Rpt Mizener, Claridge.

Schoenwald, Richard L. "FSF as John Keats." *Boston University Studies in English*, 3 (Spring 1957), 12–21.

Schwartz, Delmore. "The Dark Night of FSF." *Nation*, 172 (24 Feb 1951), 180–182.

Stallman, R W. "Conrad and *The Great Gatsby.*" *Twentieth Century Literature*, 1 (Apr 1955), 5–12. Rpt Claridge.

Tanselle, G Thomas & Jackson R Bryer. "*The Great Gatsby*—A Study in Literary Reputation." *New Mexico Quarterly*, 33 (Winter 1963–1964), 409–425. Rpt Bruccoli (1971), Claridge.

Trilling, Lionel. "F Plain." *New Yorker*, 26 (3 Feb 1951), 90–92.

Troy, William. "SF—The Authority of Failure." *Accent*, 6 (Autumn 1945), 56–60. Rpt Kazin, Mizener, Claridge.

*Watkins, Floyd C. "F's Jay Gatz and Young Ben Franklin." *New England Quarterly*, 27 (Jun 1954), 249–252. Rpt Piper.

Weir, Charles, Jr. "'An Invite With Gilded Edges.'" *Virginia Quarterly Review*, 20 (Winter 1944), 100–113. Rpt Kazin, Claridge.

Wescott, Glenway. "The Moral of SF." *New Republic,* 104 (17 Feb 1941), 213–217. Rpt Wilson, Kazin, Claridge.

Wilson, Edmund. "The Literary Spotlight—VI: FSF." *Bookman,* 55 (Mar 1922), 20–25. Rpt Kazin, Mizener, Bloom (1985), Claridge.

Young, Philip & Charles W Mann. "F's *Sun Also Rises.*" *Fitzgerald/Hemingway Annual* (1970), 1-9.

— Matthew J. Bruccoli

ERNEST HEMINGWAY
Oak Park, Ill, 21 Jul 1899–Ketchum, Idaho, 2 Jul 1961

E rnest Hemingway continues to inspire voluminous critical, biographical, and bibliographical work. His novels, short stories, and nonfiction won him international acclaim as an innovative stylist and spokesman for his generation. Critical and biographical attention to Hemingway has increased exponentially since the 1950s, when the earliest book-length studies explored his economical style, heroic code, themes of death and violence, and place in the American tradition. Rivaling his literary reputation, which earned him Pulitzer (1952) and Nobel (1954) prizes, is the public image he generated as a sportsman, war correspondent, and expatriate. Biographical scholarship, beginning in 1969, has helped distinguish the public and private Hemingways, challenging his anti-intellectual pose and encouraging a revaluation of his canon. This revaluation, prompted as well by the appearance of several posthumous works, examines Hemingway's art in terms of its social consciousness, relationship to romanticism and modernism, historical context, and pseudo-autobiographical perspective. Joining these studies are estimations of Hemingway's substantial influence, a renewed interest in his experimental work of the 1930s, and discussions of his theory of omission and aesthetic assumptions.

Bibliographies & Catalogues

American Literary Scholarship: An Annual, 1963– . Durham, NC: Duke U P, 1965– . Chapters on EH.

Bentz, Hans Willi. *EH in Übersetzungen.* Frankfurt a M: Bentz, 1963.

Catalog of the EH Collection at the John F. Kennedy Library, 2 vols. Boston: Hall, 1982.

Clarke, Graham. "H in England: Bibliography." *Hemingway Review,* 1 (Spring 1982), 76–84. Primary & secondary.

"A Comprehensive Checklist of H Short Fiction Criticism, Explication, and Commentary, 1975–1989." Benson (1990), 395–458.

*Hanneman, Audre. *EH: A Comprehensive Bibliography*. Princeton, NJ: Princeton U P, rev 1967. Primary & secondary.

*Hanneman. *Supplement to EH: A Comprehensive Bibliography*. Princeton, NJ: Princeton U P, 1975. Primary & secondary.

Hoffman, Frederick J. "EH." *Sixteen Modern American Authors: A Survey of Research and Criticism,* ed Jackson R Bryer (Durham, NC: Duke U P, 1974), 367–416.

*Larson, Kelli A. *EH: A Reference Guide, 1974–1989*. Boston: Hall, 1990. Secondary.

*Wagner, Linda Welshimer. *EH: A Reference Guide*. Boston: Hall, 1977. Secondary.

Young, Philip & Charles W Mann. *The H Manuscripts: An Inventory*. University Park: Pennsylvania State U P, 1969.

Books

Three Stories and Ten Poems. Paris: Contact Editions, 1923.

in our time. Paris: Three Mountains, 1924. Stories.

In Our Time. NY: Boni & Liveright, 1925. Stories.

The Torrents of Spring. NY: Scribners, 1926. Parody.

Today Is Friday. Englewood, NJ: As Stable, 1926. Play.

The Sun Also Rises. NY: Scribners, 1926; *Fiesta*. London: Cape, 1927. *The Sun Also Rises: A Facsimile Edition*, 2 vols. ed Matthew J Bruccoli. Detroit: Manly/Omnigraphics, 1990. Novel.

Men Without Women. NY: Scribners, 1927. Stories.

A Farewell to Arms. NY: Scribners, 1929. Novel.

Death in the Afternoon. NY: Scribners, 1932. Nonfiction.

God Rest You Merry Gentlemen. NY: House of Books, 1933. Story.

Winner Take Nothing. NY & London: Scribners, 1933. Stories.

Green Hills of Africa. NY: Scribners, 1935. Nonfiction.

To Have and Have Not. NY: Scribners, 1937. Novel.

The Spanish Earth, intro by Jasper Wood. Cleveland, Ohio: Savage, 1938. Documentary.

The Fifth Column and the First Forty-nine Stories. NY: Scribners, 1938. Play & stories.

The Fifth Column. NY: Scribners, 1940. Play.

For Whom the Bell Tolls. NY: Scribners, 1940. Novel.

Across the River and Into the Trees. NY: Scribners, 1950. Novel.

The Old Man and the Sea. NY: Scribners, 1952. Novel.

The Collected Poems. Npl: unauthorized edition, nd.

The Wild Years, ed with intro by Gene Z Hanrahan. NY: Dell, 1962. Journalism.

A Moveable Feast. NY: Scribners, 1964. Memoir.

By-Line: EH, ed with intro by William White. NY: Scribners, 1967. Articles.

The Fifth Column and Four Stories of the Spanish Civil War. NY: Scribners, 1969. Play & stories.

EH, Cub Reporter: Kansas City Star Stories, ed Bruccoli. Pittsburgh, Pa: U Pittsburgh P, 1970. Articles.

Islands in the Stream. NY: Scribners, 1970. Novel.

EH's Apprenticeship: Oak Park, 1916–1917, ed with intro by Bruccoli. Washington: NCR Microcard, 1971. High-school writings.

EH: 88 Poems, ed with intro by Nicholas Gerogiannis. NY: Bruccoli Clark/Harcourt Brace Jovanovich, 1979. Rev as *Complete Poems.* Lincoln & London: U Nebraska P, 1992.

EH on Writing, ed Larry W Phillips. NY: Scribners, 1984.

EH: Dateline: Toronto: The Complete Toronto Star Dispatches, 1920–1924, ed with intro by White; foreword by Charles Scribner, Jr. NY: Scribners, 1985.

The Dangerous Summer, intro by James A Michener. NY: Scribners, 1985. Nonfiction.

The Garden of Eden. NY: Scribners, 1986. Novel.

Letters & Diaries

"An African Journal," ed Ray Cave. *Sports Illustrated,* 35 (20 Dec 1971), 40–52, 57–66; 36 (3 Jan 1972), 26–46; 36 (10 Jan 1972), 22–30, 43–50.

EH: Selected Letters, 1917–1961, ed with intro by Carlos Baker. NY: Scribners, 1981.

Other

"The Spanish War." *Fact,* no 16 (Jul 1938). Articles.

Men at War, ed with intro by EH. NY: Crown, 1942. Stories.

Collections

The Viking Portable Library: H, intro by Malcolm Cowley. NY: Viking, 1944.

The Essential H. London: Cape, 1947.

The H Reader, foreword & prefaces by Charles Poore. NY: Scribners, 1953.

Three Novels of EH: The Sun Also Rises, intro by Cowley; *A Farewell to Arms,* intro by Robert Penn Warren; *The Old Man and the Sea,* intro by Carlos Baker. NY: Scribners, 1962.

The Nick Adams Stories, ed with intro by Philip Young. NY: Scribners, 1972.

The Enduring H, ed with intro by Charles Scribner, Jr. NY: Scribners, 1974.

The Complete Short Stories of EH: The Finca Vigía Edition. NY: Scribners, 1987

Manuscripts & Archives

The major collections are at the John F Kennedy Library; the U of Delaware Library; the U of Virginia Library; Princeton U Library; Stanford U Library; the Harry Ransom Humanities Research Center, U of Texas, Austin; & the Lilly Library, Indiana U.

Biographies

BOOKS

Arnold, Lloyd R. *High on the Wild With H.* Caldwell, Idaho: Caxton, 1968.

*Baker, Carlos. *EH: A Life Story.* NY: Scribners, 1969.

Bruccoli, Matthew J. *Scott and Ernest.* NY: Random House, 1978.

Buckley, Peter. *Ernest.* NY: Dial, 1978. Pictorial biography.

Burgess, Anthony. *EH and His World.* NY: Scribners, 1978.

Castillo-Pauché, José Luis. *H in Spain,* trans Helen R Lane. Garden City, NY: Doubleday, 1974.

Conrad, Barnaby. *H's Spain,* photos by Loomis Dean (San Francisco: Chronicle, 1989). Pictorial biography.

*Donaldson, Scott. *By Force of Will: The Life and Art of EH.* NY: Viking, 1977.

Donnell, David. *H in Toronto*. Windsor, Ont: Black Moss, 1982.

Fuentes, Norberto. *H in Cuba*, ed Larry Alson; intro by Gabriel García Márquez. Secaucus, NJ: Stuart, 1984.

Fuentes. *EH: Rediscovered*, photos by Roberta Herrera Sontolongo. NY: Scribners, 1988.

*Griffin, Peter. *Along With Youth: H, the Early Years*, foreword by Jack Hemingway. NY: Oxford U P, 1985.

*Griffin. *Less Than a Treason: H in Paris*. NY: Oxford U P, 1990.

Hemingway, Gregory. *Papa: A Personal Memoir*, preface by Norman Mailer. Boston: Houghton Mifflin, 1976.

Hemingway, Jack. *Misadventures of a Fly Fisherman: My Life With and Without Papa*. Dallas, Tex: Taylor, 1986.

Hemingway, Leicester. *My Brother, EH*. Cleveland, Ohio: World, 1962.

Hemingway, Mary. *How It Was*. NY: Knopf, 1976.

Hotchner, A E. *Papa H*. NY: Random House, 1966. Augmented ed, NY: Quill, 1983.

Hotchner. *H and His World*. NY: Vendome, 1989. Pictorial biography.

Kert, Bernice. *The H Women*. NY: Norton, 1983.

Lania, Leo. *H: A Pictorial Biography*. NY: Viking, 1961.

McLendon, James. *Papa: H in Key West*. Miami, Fla: Seemann, 1972.

Mellow, James R. *H: A Life Without Consequences*. Boston: Houghton Mifflin, 1992.

*Meyers, Jeffrey. *H: A Biography*. NY: Harper & Row, 1985.

Miller, Madelaine H. *Ernie: H's Sister "Sunny" Remembers*, preface by Robert Traver. NY: Crown, 1975.

Montgomery, Constance Cappel. *H in Michigan*. NY: Fleet, 1966.

Nelson, Raymond S. *EH: Life, Work, and Criticism*. Fredericton, NB: York, 1984.

*Reynolds, Michael. *The Young H*. NY: Blackwell, 1986.

*Reynolds. *H: The Paris Years*. Cambridge, Mass: Blackwell, 1989.

*Reynolds. *H: An Annotated Chronology*. Detroit: Manly/Omnigraphics, 1991.

*Reynolds. *H: The American Homecoming*. Cambridge, Mass: Blackwell, 1992.

Samuelson, Arnold. *With H: A Year in Key West and Cuba*. NY: Random House, 1984.

Sanford, Marcelline Hemingway. *At the Hemingways*. Boston: Atlantic/Little, Brown, 1962.

Stanton, Edward F. *H and Spain: A Pursuit*. Seattle: U Washington P, 1989.

Villard, Henry S & James Nagel. *H in Love and War: The Lost Diary of Agnes von Kurowsky, Her Letters, and Correspondence of EH.* Boston: Northeastern U P, 1989.

BOOK SECTIONS

Callaghan, Morley. *That Summer in Paris* (NY: Coward-McCann, 1963), passim.

Donnelly, Honoria M. *Sara and Gerald* (NY: Times, 1982), passim.

Dos Passos, John. *The Best Times* (NY: NAL, 1966), passim.

Loeb, Harold. "England, France, and H." *The Way It Was* (NY: Criterion, 1959), 209–220.

ARTICLES

Bishop, John Peale. "Homage to H." *New Republic,* 89 (11 Nov 1936), 39–42. Rpt *After the Genteel Tradition,* ed Malcolm Cowley (NY: Norton, 1937).

*Cowley, Malcolm. "A Portrait of Mister Papa." *Life,* 26 (10 Jan 1949), 86–90, 93–94, 96–98, 100–101. Rev & rpt McCaffery.

Donaldson, Scott. "The Wooing of EH." *American Literature,* 53 (Jan 1982), 691–710.

Donaldson. "Dos and Hem: A Literary Friendship." *Centennial Review,* 29 (Spring 1985), 163–185. Rpt Wagner (1987).

Doyle, N Ann & Neal B Huston. "EH's Letters to Adriana Ivancich." *Library Chronicle of the University of Texas,* ns 30 (1985), 15–37.

Eastman, Max. "The Great and Small in EH." *Saturday Review,* 42 (4 Apr 1959), 13–15, 50–51. Rpt *Great Companions* by Eastman (NY: Farrar, Straus & Cudahy, 1959).

Kubie, Lawrence. "A Suppressed Essay on EH," ed with intro by Jeffrey Meyers. *American Imago,* 41 (Spring 1984), 1–18.

Loeb, Harold. "H's Bitterness." *Connecticut Review,* 1 (Oct 1967), 7–24.

MacLeish, Archibald. "His Mirror Was Danger." *Life,* 51 (14 Jul 1961), 71–73.

Meyers, Jeffrey. "H, Ford Madox Ford, and *A Moveable Feast.*" *Critical Quarterly,* 25 (Winter 1983), 35–42.

Meyers. "H's Second War: The Greco–Turkish Conflict, 1920–1922." *Modern Fiction Studies,* 30 (Spring 1984), 25–36.

Miller, Linda P. "Gerald Murphy and EH: Part I." *Studies in American Fiction,* 12 (Autumn 1984), 129–144.

Miller. "Gerald Murphy and EH: Part II." *Studies in American Fiction,* 13 (Spring 1985), 1–13.

Pizer, Donald. "The H–Dos Passos Relationship." *Journal of Modern Literature,* 13 (Mar 1986), 111–128.

Reynolds, Michael S. "H's Home: Depression and Suicide." *American Literature,* 57 (Dec 1985), 600–610. Rpt Wagner (1987).

Spilka, Mark. "Victorian Keys to the Early H: Part I—*John Halifax, Gentleman.*" *Journal of Modern Literature,* 10 (Mar 1983), 125–150.

Spilka. "Victorian Keys to the Early H: Part II—*Fauntleroy* and *Finn.*" *Journal of Modern Literature,* 10 (Jun 1983), 289–310.

Spilka. "Victorian Keys to the Early H: Captain Marryat." *Novel,* 17 (Winter 1984), 116–140.

Interviews

BOOK

*Bruccoli, Matthew J, ed. *Conversations With EH.* Jackson: U P Mississippi, 1986.

ARTICLES

Plimpton, George. "The Art of Fiction XXI: EH." *Paris Review,* no 18 (Spring 1958), 60–89. Rpt Baker (1961). Rpt *Writers at Work, Second Series,* ed Plimpton (NY: Viking, 1963). Rpt Bruccoli (1986).

Ross, Lillian. "How Do You Like It Now, Gentlemen?" *New Yorker,* 26 (13 May 1950), 36–38, 40–46, 48–62. Rpt *Portrait of H* by Ross (NY: Simon & Schuster, 1961). Rpt *Reporting* by Ross (NY: Simon & Schuster, 1964). Rpt Weeks.

Critical Studies

BOOKS

Atkins, John. *The Art of EH: His Work and Personality.* London: Nevill, 1952.

*Baker, Carlos. *H: The Writer as Artist.* Princeton, NJ: Princeton U P, rev 1972.

Baker, Sheridan. *EH: An Introduction and Interpretation.* NY: Holt, Rinehart & Winston, 1967.

Beegel, Susan F. *H's Craft of Omission: Four Manuscript Examples.* Ann Arbor, Mich: UMI, 1988.

*Benson, Jackson J. *H: The Writer's Art of Self-Defense.* Minneapolis: U Minnesota P, 1969.

Brasch, James D & Joseph Sigman. *H's Library: A Composite Record.* NY: Garland, 1981.

Brenner, Gerry. *Concealments in H's Work.* Columbus: Ohio State U P, 1983.

Brenner. *The Old Man and the Sea: Story of a Common Man.* NY: Twayne, 1991

Broer, Lawrence R. *H's Spanish Tragedy.* University: U Alabama P, 1973.

Capellán, Angel. *H and the Hispanic World.* Ann Arbor, Mich: UMI, 1985.

Cooper, Stephen. *The Politics of EH.* Ann Arbor, Mich: UMI, 1987.

DeFalco, Joseph. *The Hero in H's Short Stories.* Pittsburgh, Pa: U Pittsburgh P, 1963.

Fellner, Harriet. *H as Playwright: The Fifth Column.* Ann Arbor, Mich: UMI, 1986.

Fenton, Charles A. *The Apprenticeship of EH.* NY: Farrar, Straus & Young, 1954.

Flora, Joseph M. *H's Nick Adams.* Baton Rouge: Louisiana State U P, 1982.

Gaggin, John. *H and Nineteenth-Century Aestheticism.* Ann Arbor, Mich: UMI, 1988.

Gajdusek, Robert E. *H and Joyce: A Study in Debt and Payment.* Corte Madera, Calif: Square Circle, 1984.

Grebstein, Sheldon Norman. *H's Craft.* Carbondale: Southern Illinois U P, 1973.

Grimes, Larry E. *The Religious Design of H's Early Fiction.* Ann Arbor, Mich: UMI, 1985.

Gurko, Leo. *EH and the Pursuit of Heroism.* NY: Crowell, 1968.

Hovey, Richard B. *H: The Inward Terrain.* Seattle: U Washington P, 1968.

Joost, Nicholas. *EH and the Little Magazines: The Paris Years.* Barre, Mass: Barre, 1968.

Killinger, John. *H and the Dead Gods: A Study in Existentialism.* Lexington: U Kentucky P, 1960.

Kobler, J F. *EH: Journalist and Artist.* Ann Arbor, Mich: UMI, 1985.

Laurence, Frank M. *H and the Movies.* Jackson: U P Mississippi, 1981.

Lewis, Robert W, Jr. *H on Love.* Austin: U Texas P, 1965.

Lewis. *A Farewell to Arms: The War of the Words.* NY: Twayne, 1992.

Messent, Peter. *EH.* NY: St Martin, 1992.

Nahal, Chaman. *The Narrative Pattern in EH's Fiction.* Rutherford, NJ: Fairleigh Dickinson U P, 1971.

Nelson, Ray. *H: Expressionist Artist.* Ames: Iowa State U P, 1979.

Oldsey, Bernard. *H's Hidden Craft: The Writing of A Farewell to Arms.* University Park: Pennsylvania State U P, 1979.

Peterson, Richard K. *H: Direct and Oblique.* The Hague: Mouton, 1969.

Phillips, Gene D. *H and Film.* NY: Ungar, 1980.

*Raeburn, John. *Fame Became of Him: H as Public Writer.* Bloomington: Indiana U P, 1984.

*Reynolds, Michael S. *H's First War: The Making of A Farewell to Arms.* Princeton, NJ: Princeton U P, 1976.

Reynolds. *H's Reading, 1910–1940: An Inventory.* Princeton, NJ: Princeton U P, 1981.

Reynolds. *The Sun Also Rises: A Novel of the Twenties.* Boston: Twayne, 1988.

*Rovit, Earl & Gerry Brenner. *EH.* Boston: Twayne, 1986.

*Smith, Paul. *A Reader's Guide to the Short Stories of EH.* Boston: Hall, 1989.

*Stephens, Robert O. *H's Nonfiction.* Chapel Hill: U North Carolina P, 1968.

Sutherland, Fraser. *The Style of Innocence: A Study of H and Callaghan.* Toronto: Clarke, Irwin, 1972.

Svoboda, Frederic J. *H and The Sun Also Rises: The Crafting of a Style.* Lawrence: U P Kansas, 1983.

Tetlow, Wendolyn E. *H's In Our Time: Lyrical Dimensions.* Lewisburg, Pa: Bucknell U P, 1992.

Waldhorn, Arthur. *A Reader's Guide to EH.* NY: Farrar, Straus & Giroux, 1972.

Watts, Emily Stipes. *EH and the Arts.* Urbana: U Illinois P, 1971.

Weber, Ronald. *H's Art of Non-Fiction.* NY: St Martin, 1990.

Whitlow, Roger. *Cassandra's Daughters: The Women in H.* Westport, Conn: Greenwood, 1984.

Williams, Wirt. *The Tragic Art of EH.* Baton Rouge: Louisiana State U P, 1981.

Wylder, Delbert E. *H's Heroes.* Albuquerque: U New Mexico P, 1969.

Young, Philip. *EH*. Minneapolis: U Minnesota P, 1965.

*Young. *EH: A Reconsideration*. University Park: Pennsylvania State U P, rev 1966.

COLLECTIONS OF ESSAYS

Asselineau, Roger, ed. *The Literary Reputation of H in Europe*. NY: NYU P, 1965.

Astro, Richard & Jackson J Benson, eds. *H in Our Time*. Corvallis: Oregon State U P, 1974.

Baker, Carlos, ed. *H and His Critics: An International Anthology*. NY: Hill & Wang, 1961.

*Baker, ed. *EH: Critiques of Four Major Novels*. NY: Scribners, 1962.

Beegel, Susan F, ed. *H's Neglected Short Fiction: New Perspectives*. Ann Arbor, Mich: UMI, 1989.

*Benson, Jackson J, ed. *The Short Stories of EH: Critical Essays*. Durham, NC: Duke U P, 1975.

*Benson, ed. *New Critical Approaches to the Short Stories of EH*. Durham, NC: Duke U P, 1990.

Bloom, Harold, ed. *Modern Critical Views: EH*. NY: Chelsea House, 1985.

Bloom, ed. *EH's The Sun Also Rises*. NY: Chelsea House, 1987.

Bloom, ed. *EH's A Farewell to Arms*. NY: Chelsea House, 1987.

Bloom, ed. *Brett Ashley*. NY: Chelsea House, 1991.

Donaldson, Scott, ed. *New Essays on A Farewell to Arms*. NY: Cambridge U P, 1990.

Gellens, Jay, ed. *Twentieth Century Interpretations of A Farewell to Arms*. Englewood Cliffs, NJ: Prentice-Hall, 1970.

Graham, John, ed. *The Merrill Studies in A Farewell to Arms*. Columbus, Ohio: Merrill, 1971.

Grebstein, Sheldon Norman, ed. *The Merrill Studies in For Whom the Bell Tolls*. Columbus, Ohio: Merrill, 1971.

Howell, John M, ed. *H's African Stories: The Stories, Their Sources, the Critics*. NY: Scribners, 1969.

Jobes, Katharine T, ed. *Twentieth Century Interpretations of The Old Man and the Sea*. Englewood Cliffs, NJ: Prentice-Hall, 1968.

Lee, A Robert, ed. *EH: New Critical Essays*. Totowa, NJ: Barnes & Noble, 1983.

Lewis, Robert W, ed. *H in Italy and Other Essays*. NY: Praeger, 1990.

McCaffery, John K M, ed. *EH: The Man and His Work.* Cleveland, Ohio: World, 1950.

*Meyers, Jeffrey, ed. *H: The Critical Heritage.* London: Routledge & Kegan Paul, 1982.

Nagel, James, ed. *EH: The Writer in Context.* Madison: U Wisconsin P, 1984.

Noble, Donald R, ed. *H: A Revaluation.* Troy, NY: Whitston, 1983.

*Oldsey, Bernard, ed. *EH: The Papers of a Writer.* NY: Garland, 1981.

Reynolds, Michael S, ed. *Critical Essays on EH's In Our Time.* Boston: Hall, 1983.

Ryan, Frank L, ed. *The Immediate Critical Reception of EH.* Washington: U P America, 1980.

Sanderson, Rena, ed. *Blowing the Bridge: Essays on H and For Whom the Bell Tolls.* NY: Greenwood, 1992.

Sarason, Bertram D, ed. *H and The Sun Set.* Washington: NCR/Microcard, 1972.

*Scafella, Frank, ed. *H: Essays of Reassessment.* NY: Oxford U P, 1991.

Stephens, Robert O, ed. *EH: The Critical Reception.* Npl: Franklin, 1977.

Wagner, Linda Welshimer, ed. *EH: Five Decades of Criticism.* East Lansing: Michigan State U P, 1974.

*Wagner, ed. *EH: Six Decades of Criticism.* East Lansing: Michigan State U P, 1987.

Wagner-Martin, Linda, ed. *New Essays on The Sun Also Rises.* NY: Cambridge U P, 1987.

Waldhorn, Arthur, ed. *EH: A Collection of Criticism.* NY: McGraw-Hill, 1973. Includes checklist.

Waldmeir, Joseph J & Kenneth Marek, eds. *Up in Michigan: Proceedings of the First National Conference of the Hemingway Society.* East Lansing: Michigan State U P, 1984.

Weeks, Robert P, ed. *H: A Collection of Critical Essays.* Englewood Cliffs, NJ: Prentice-Hall, 1962.

White, William, ed. *The Merrill Studies in The Sun Also Rises.* Columbus, Ohio: Merrill, 1969.

SPECIAL JOURNALS

Arizona Quarterly, 33 (Summer 1977). EH issue.

Arizona Quarterly, 39 (Summer 1983). EH issue.

Arizona Quarterly, 41 (Winter 1985). EH issue.

Arizona Quarterly, 44 (Summer 1988). EH issue.

Clockwatch Review, 3, no 2 (1986). EH issue.

College Literature, 7 (Fall 1980). EH issue.

Fitzgerald/Hemingway Annual (1969–1979). Washington: Microcard Editions, 1969–1976; Detroit: Bruccoli Clark/Gale, 1977–1979. Includes checklists.

Hemingway Notes (1971–1974, 1979–1981).

Hemingway Review (1981–). Includes checklists.

Modern Fiction Studies, 1 (Aug 1955). EH issue.

Modern Fiction Studies, 14 (Autumn 1968). EH issue.

Mark Twain Journal, 11 (Summer 1962). EH issue.

North Dakota Quarterly, 60 (Spring 1992). EH/André Malraux issue.

Saturday Review, 44 (29 Jul 1961). EH issue.

Student (Wake Forrest U) (Winter 1978). EH issue.

BOOK SECTIONS

Aldridge, John W. "H: Nightmare and the Correlative of Loss," "The Neo-Hemingways: and the Failure of Protest." *After the Lost Generation* (NY: McGraw-Hill, 1951), 23–43, 107–116.

Aldridge. "Afterthoughts of the Twenties and *The Sun Also Rises.*" Wagner-Martin, 109–129.

Beach, Joseph Warren. "EH: Empirical Ethics," "EH: The Aesthetics of Simplicity." *American Fiction, 1920–1940* (NY: Macmillan, 1941), 69–93, 97–119.

Brasch, James D. "Invention From Knowledge: The H-Cowley Correspondence." Nagel, 201–236.

Bridgman, Richard. "EH." *The Colloquial Style in America* (NY: Oxford U P, 1966), 195–230. Rpt Wagner (1974).

*Brooks, Cleanth. "EH: Man on His Moral Uppers." *The Hidden God: Studies in H, Faulkner, Yeats, Eliot, and Warren* (New Haven: Yale U P, 1963), 6–21.

Davidson, Arnold E & Cathy N. "Decoding the H Hero in *The Sun Also Rises.*" Wagner-Martin, 83–107.

Donaldson, Scott. "Humor in *The Sun Also Rises.*" Wagner-Martin, 19–41.

Fishkin, Shelly Fisher. "EH." *From Fact to Fiction* (Baltimore, Md: Johns Hopkins U P, 1985), 135–164, 243–249.

Lehan, Richard. "H Among the Moderns." Astro & Benson, 191–212.

Lewis, Robert W, Jr. "The Making of *Death in the Afternoon*." Nagel, 31–52.

Martin, Wendy. "Brett Ashley as New Woman in *The Sun Also Rises*." Wagner-Martin, 65–82.

O'Faolain, Sean. "EH: or Men Without Memories." *The Vanishing Hero* (London: Eyre/Spottiswoode, 1956), 137–165.

Plimpton, George. "Dissenting Opinion." *Against the American Grain* by Dwight Macdonald (NY: Random House, 1962), 179–184.

Reynolds, Michael S. "The *Sun* and Its Time: Recovering the Historical Context." Wagner-Martin, 43–64.

Scholes, Robert. "Decoding Papa: 'A Very Short Story' as Work and Text." *Semiotics and Interpretation* (New Haven: Yale U P, 1982), 110–126. Rpt Benson (1990).

*Smith, Paul. "A Partial Review: Critical Essays on the Short Stories, 1976–1989." Benson (1990), 375–391.

Spilka, Mark. "The Death of Love in *The Sun Also Rises*." *Twelve Original Essays on Great American Novels,* ed Charles Shapiro (Detroit: Wayne State U P, 1958), 238–256. Rpt Baker (1961), Baker (1962), Weeks.

Van Antwerp, Margaret A, ed. "EH." *Dictionary of Literary Biography Documentary Series,* Vol 1 (Detroit: Bruccoli Clark/Gale, 1982), 291–360.

Watkins, Floyd C. *"The Sun Also Rises* and the Failure of Language," "World Pessimism and Personal Cheeriness in *A Farewell to Arms*," "H's First 'Big Writing,'" "Garrulous Patriot," "The Iceberg and the Cardboard Box." *The Flesh and the Word: Eliot, H, and Faulkner* (Nashville, Tenn: Vanderbilt U P, 1971), 95–166.

Way, Brian. "H the Intellectual: A Version of Modernism." Lee, 151–171.

ARTICLES

Bishop, John Peale. "The Missing All." *Virginia Quarterly Review,* 13 (Winter 1937), 106–121. Rpt McCaffery.

Bredahl, A Carl. "The Body as Matrix: Narrative Pattern in *Green Hills of Africa*." *Midwest Quarterly,* 28 (Summer 1987), 455–472.

Brenner, Gerry. "Are We Going to H's *Feast?*" *American Literature,* 54 (Dec 1982), 528–544. Rpt Wagner (1987).

Bromwich, David. "H's Valor." *Grand Street,* 7 (Winter 1988), 185–217.

Burhans, Clinton S, Jr. "The Complex Unity of *In Our Time*." *Modern Fiction Studies,* 14 (Autumn 1968), 313–328. Rpt Reynolds (1983).

Coleman, Arthur. "H's *The Spanish Earth.*" *Hemingway Review,* 2 (Fall 1982), 64–67.

*Cowley, Malcolm. "H at Midnight." *New Republic,* 111 (14 Aug 1944), 190, 192, 194–195. Expanded as intro to *The Viking Portable Library: H.* Rpt *The Flower and the Leaf* by Cowley (NY: Viking, 1985).

Cowley. "H's Wound—and Its Consequences for American Literature." *Georgia Review,* 38 (Summer 1984), 223–239.

Eastman, Max. "Bull in the Afternoon." *New Republic,* 125 (7 Jun 1933), 94–97. Rpt *Art and the Life of Action* by Eastman (NY: Knopf, 1934). Rpt McCaffery.

*Fitzgerald, F Scott. "How to Waste Material." *Bookman,* 63 (May 1926), 262–265. Rpt *Afternoon of an Author,* ed Arthur Mizener (Princeton, NJ: Princeton U Library, 1957).

Flanagan, John T. "H's Debt to Sherwood Anderson." *Journal of English and Germanic Philology,* 54 (Oct 1955), 507–520.

*Fuchs, Daniel. "EH, Literary Critic." *American Literature,* 36 (Jan 1965), 431–451. Rpt Waldhorn.

Geismar, Maxwell. "No Man Alone Now." *Virginia Quarterly Review,* 17 (Autumn 1941), 517–534. Rev as "EH: You Could Always Come Back." *Writers in Crisis* by Geismar (Boston: Houghton Mifflin, 1942). Rpt McCaffery.

Halliday, E M. "H's Ambiguity: Symbolism and Irony." *American Literature,* 28 (Mar 1956), 1–22. Rpt Baker (1962), Weeks.

Hinkle, James. "'Dear Mr. Scribner'—About the Published Text of *The Sun Also Rises.*" *Hemingway Review,* 6 (Fall 1986), 43–64.

Hinz, Evelyn J & John J Teunissen. "*Islands in the Stream* as H's *Laocoön.*" *Contemporary Literature,* 29 (Spring 1988), 26–48.

Josephs, Allen. "*Death in the Afternoon:* A Reconsideration." *Hemingway Review,* 2 (Fall 1982), 2–16.

*Levin, Harry. "Observations on the Style of EH." *Kenyon Review,* 13 (Autumn 1951), 581–609. Rpt *Contexts of Criticism* by Levin (Cambridge, Mass: Harvard U P, 1957). Rpt Weeks.

Lewis, Robert W, Jr & Max Westbrook. "The Texas Manuscript of 'The Snows of Kilimanjaro.'" *Texas Quarterly,* 9 (Winter 1966), 65–101.

Lewis & Westbrook. "'The Snows of Kilimanjaro': Collated and Annotated." *Texas Quarterly,* 13 (Summer 1970), 67–143.

Lewis, Wyndham. "The Dumb Ox: A Study of EH." *Life & Letters,* 10 (Apr 1934), 33–45. Rpt *Men Without Art* by Lewis (London: Cassell, 1934).

Lisca, Peter. "The Structure of H's *Across the River and Into the Trees.*" *Modern Fiction Studies,* 12 (Summer 1966), 232–250.

Lounsberry, Barbara. "*Green Hills of Africa:* H's Celebration of Memory." *Hemingway Review,* 2 (Spring 1983), 23–31.

Magaw, Malcolm O. "The Fusion of History and Immediacy: H's Artist-Hero in *The Garden of Eden.*" *CLIO,* 17 (Fall 1987), 21–36.

Monteiro, George. "EH, Psalmist." *Journal of Modern Literature,* 14 (Summer 1987), 83–95.

O'Hara, John. "The Author's Name Is H." *New York Times Book Review* (10 Sep 1950), 1, 30–31.

O'Sullivan, Sibbie. "Love and Friendship/Man and Woman in *The Sun Also Rises.*" *Arizona Quarterly,* 44 (Summer 1988), 76–97.

Reynolds, Michael S. "Words Killed, Wounded, Missing in Action." *Hemingway Notes,* 6 (Spring 1981), 2–9.

Reynolds. "A Supplement to *H's Reading, 1910–1940.*" *Studies in American Fiction,* 14 (Spring 1986), 99–108.

Ryan, Steven T. "Prosaic Unity in *To Have and Have Not.*" *Hemingway Review,* 4 (Fall 1984), 27–32.

Smith, Paul. "H's Early Manuscripts: The Theory and Practice of Omission." *Journal of Modern Literature,* 10 (Jun 1983), 268–288.

Smith. "H's Apprentice Fiction: 1919–1921." *American Literature,* 58 (Dec 1986), 574–588. Rpt Benson (1990).

Spilka, Mark. "H's Barbershop Quintet: The *Garden of Eden* Manuscript." *Novel,* 21 (Fall 1987), 29–55.

Wagner, Linda W. "'Proud and Friendly and Gently': Women in H's Early Fiction." *College Literature,* 7 (Fall 1980), 238–247.

*Warren, Robert Penn. "H." *Kenyon Review,* 9 (Winter 1947), 1–28. Rpt as intro to *A Farewell to Arms* (NY: Scribners, 1949). Rpt *Selected Essays* by Warren (NY: Random House, 1958).

Wilson, Edmund. "Mr. H's Dry Points." *Dial,* 77 (Oct 1924), 340–341. Augmented as "Emergence of EH." *The Shores of Light* by Wilson (NY: Farrar, Straus & Young, 1952). Rpt Baker (1961).

Wilson. "The Sportsman's Tragedy." *New Republic,* 53 (14 Dec 1927), 102–103. Rpt *The Shores of Light* by Wilson (NY: Farrar, Straus & Young, 1952).

*Wilson. "EH: Bourdon Gauge of Morale." *Atlantic,* 164 (Jul 1939), 36–46. Rpt as "H: Gauge of Morale." *The Wound and the Bow* by Wilson (NY: Oxford U P, 1947). Rpt McCaffery.

— *Albert J. DeFazio, III*

JOHN STEINBECK

Salinas, Calif, 27 Feb 1902–New York City, NY, 20 Dec 1968

Throughout his career John Steinbeck had an easier relationship with the reading public than with literary critics. Readers liked the accessibility of his prose; critics, while recognizing the power of *The Grapes of Wrath* and the other fiction of the 1930s, often found later books simplistic, sentimental, or overly stylized. However uneven Steinbeck's work is, few deny him a significant place in twentieth-century literature. At his best in the 1930s and early 1940s, he wrote compassionately about common people and thoughtfully about the environment. While criticism in the 1940s and 1950s focused on the social and political issues depicted in his early fiction, more recent scholarship has given increased attention to his later works, as well as to his lucid prose, his literary sources, and his artistic vision. Steinbeck was awarded the Nobel Prize for Literature in 1962.

Bibliographies & Catalogues

*Goldstone, Adrian H & John R Payne. *JS: A Bibliographical Catalogue of the Adrian H Goldstone Collection.* Austin: Humanities Research Center, U Texas, 1974. Primary.

Harmon, Robert B. *S Bibliographies: An Annotated Guide.* Metuchen, NJ: Scarecrow, 1987.

Harmon. *The Grapes of Wrath: A Fifty Year Bibliographic Survey.* San Jose, Calif: Steinbeck Research Center, 1990. Primary & secondary.

Hayashi, Tetsumaro. *A New S Bibliography, 1929–1971.* Metuchen, NJ: Scarecrow, 1973. Primary & secondary.

Hayashi. *A New S Bibliography, 1971–1981.* Metuchen, NJ: Scarecrow, 1983. Primary & secondary.

Morrow, Bradford, ed. *JS: A Collection of Books and Manuscripts Formed by Harry Valentine of Pacific Grove, California.* Santa Barbara, Calif: Morrow, 1980. Primary.

Books

Cup of Gold: A Life of Henry Morgan, Buccaneer, With Occasional Reference to History. NY: McBride, 1929. Novel.

The Pastures of Heaven. NY: Brewer, Warren & Putnam, 1932. Novel.

To a God Unknown. NY: Ballou, 1933. Novel.

Tortilla Flat. NY: Covici-Friede, 1935. Novel.

In Dubious Battle. NY: Covici-Friede, 1936. Novel.

Nothing So Monstrous. NY: Pynsan Printers, 1936. Story.

Saint Katy, the Virgin. NY: Covici-Friede, 1936. Story.

Of Mice and Men. NY: Covici-Friede, 1937. Novel.

The Red Pony. NY: Covici-Friede, 1937. Stories.

Of Mice and Men: A Play in Three Acts. NY: Covici-Friede, 1937.

The Long Valley. NY: Viking, 1938. Stories.

"Their Blood Is Strong." San Francisco: Simon J Lubin Society of California, 1938. Nonfiction.

The Grapes of Wrath. NY: Viking, 1939. Novel.

The Forgotten Village. NY: Viking, 1941. Filmscript with photographs.

Sea of Cortez: A Leisurely Journal of Travel and Research, with Edward F Ricketts. NY: Viking, 1941.

Bombs Away: The Story of a Bomber Team, photographs by John Swope. NY: Viking, 1942. Nonfiction.

The Moon Is Down: A Novel. NY: Viking, 1942.

The Moon Is Down: A Play in Two Parts. NY: Viking, 1942; NY: Dramatists Play Service, 1942.

How Edith McGillicuddy Met R. L. S. Cleveland, Ohio: Rowfant Club, 1943. Story.

Cannery Row. NY: Viking, 1945. Novel.

The Red Pony. NY: Viking, 1945. Stories.

The Wayward Bus. NY: Viking, 1947. Novel.

The Pearl. NY: Viking, 1947. Novel.

A Russian Journal, photographs & chapter by Robert Capa. NY: Viking, 1948. Nonfiction.

Burning Bright: A Play in Story Form. NY: Viking, 1950.

Burning Bright: A Play in Three Acts. NY: Dramatists Play Service, 1951.

The Log From the Sea of Cortez. NY: Viking, 1951. Nonfiction.

East of Eden. NY: Viking, 1952. Novel.

Sweet Thursday. NY: Viking, 1954. Novel.

The Short Reign of Pippin IV, a Fabrication. NY: Viking, 1957. Novel.

Once There Was a War. NY: Viking, 1958. Journalism.

The Winter of Our Discontent. NY: Viking, 1961. Novel.

Travels With Charley in Search of America. NY: Viking, 1962. Nonfiction.

Speech Accepting the Nobel Prize for Literature: Stockholm, December 10, 1962. NY: Viking, 1963.

America and Americans. NY: Viking, 1966. Nonfiction.

Viva Zapata! ed with intro by Robert E Morsberger. NY: Viking, 1975. Screenplay.

The Acts of King Arthur and His Noble Knights: From the Winchester MSS. of Thomas Malory and Other Sources, ed Chase Horton; intro by JS, NY: Farrar, Straus & Giroux, 1976. Transcription, including 72 JS letters.

Uncollected Stories of JS, ed Kiyoshi Nakayama. Tokyo: Nan Un-Do, 1986.

The Harvest Gypsies: On the Road to The Grapes of Wrath, intro Charles Wollenberg. Berkeley, Calif: Heyday, 1988. Articles.

Zapata, the Little Tiger. Covelo, Calif: Yolla Bolly, 1991. Introduction, commentary & early screenplay.

Letters, Diaries, Notebooks

A Letter Written in Reply to a Request for a Statement About His Ancestry. . . . Stamford, Conn: Overbrook, 1940.

The First Watch. San Francisco: Ritchie, 1947. Letter.

Journal of a Novel: The East of Eden Letters. NY: Viking, 1969.

S: A Life in Letters, ed with notes by Elaine Steinbeck & Robert Wallsten. NY: Viking, 1975.

Letters to Elizabeth: A Selection of Letters From JS to Elizabeth Otis, ed Florian J Shasky & Susan F Riggs; intro by Carlton Sheffield. San Francisco: Book Club of California, 1978.

S and Covici: The Story of a Friendship, ed Thomas Fensch. Middlebury, Vt: Eriksson, 1979.

Working Days: The Journals of The Grapes of Wrath, 1938–1941, ed Robert DeMott. NY: Viking, 1989.

Editions & Collections

The Viking Portable Library S, ed Pascal Covici. NY: Viking, 1943. Repub as *The Portable S,* ed Covici. NY: Viking, 1946. Repub as *The Portable S,* ed with intro by Pascal Covici, Jr. NY: Viking, 1971.

The S Pocket Book. Philadelphia: Blakiston, 1943.

The S Omnibus. London & c: Heinemann, 1950.
The Short Novels of JS, intro by Joseph Henry Jackson. NY: Viking, 1953.
S Collection, 12 vols. London: Heron, 1971.
The Grapes of Wrath: Text and Criticism, ed Peter Lisca. NY: Viking, 1972.
JS: The Grapes of Wrath, The Moon Is Down, Cannery Row, East of Eden, Of Mice and Men. London: Octopus/Heinemann, 1976.

Manuscripts & Archives

The major collections are at the Harry Ransom Humanities Research Center, U of Texas, Austin; Stanford U Library; U of Virginia Library; U of California, Berkeley, Library; Ball State U Library; John Steinbeck Library, Salinas, Calif; the Steinbeck Research Center, San Jose State U; Columbia Library; & Pierpont Morgan Library, New York City.

Biographies

BOOKS

Ariss, Bruce. *Inside Cannery Row.* Npl: Lexikos, 1988.
*Benson, Jackson J. *The True Adventures of JS, Writer.* NY: Viking, 1984.
*Benson. *Looking for S's Ghost.* Norman: U Oklahoma P, 1988.
Enea, Sparky (as told to Audry Lynch). *With S in the Sea of Cortez.* Los Osos, Calif: Sand River, 1991.
Ferrell, Keith. *JS: The Voice of the Land.* NY: Evans, 1986.
O'Connor, Richard. *JS.* NY: McGraw-Hill, 1970.
St Pierre, Brian. *JS: The California Years.* San Francisco: Chronicle, 1983.
*Valjean, Nelson. *JS: The Errant Knight: An Intimate Biography of His California Years.* San Francisco: Chronicle, 1975.

BOOK SECTIONS

Gannett, Lewis. "JS's Way of Writing." *The Portable Steinbeck* (NY: Viking, 1946), vii–xxviii.
*Larsen, Stephen & Robin. *A Fire in the Mind: The Life of Joseph Campbell* (NY: Doubleday, 1991), passim.
Lisca, Peter. "JS: A Literary Biography." Tedlock & Wicker, 3–22.
*Lorentz, Pare. *FDR's Moviemaker: Memoirs and Scripts* (Reno: U Nevada P, 1992), 105–148.

ARTICLES

Jackson, Joseph Henry. "JS: A Portrait." *Saturday Review of Literature,* 16 (25 Sep 1937), 11–12, 18.

*Schulberg, Budd. "S at the End of the Road." *Tropic—Miami Herald Sunday Magazine,* 3 (9 Feb 1969), 8–10, 12. Rpt *The Four Seasons of Success* by Schulberg (Garden City, NY: Doubleday, 1972).

Shaw, Peter. "S: The Shape of a Career." *Saturday Review,* 52 (8 Feb 1969), 10–14, 50.

Interviews

BOOK

*Fensch, Thomas, ed. *Conversations With JS.* Jackson: U P Mississippi, 1988.

Critical Studies

BOOKS

*Astro, Richard. *JS and Edward F Ricketts: The Shaping of a Novelist.* Minneapolis: U Minnesota P, 1973.

*Coers, Donald V. *JS as Propagandist: The Moon Is Down Goes to War.* Tuscaloosa: U Alabama P, 1991.

DeMott, Robert J. *S's Reading: A Catalogue of Books Owned and Borrowed.* NY: Garland, 1984.

Ditsky, John. *Essays on East of Eden.* Muncie, Ind: JS Society of America, Ball State U, 1977.

*Fontenrose, Joseph. *JS: An Introduction and Interpretation.* NY: Barnes & Noble, 1963.

*French, Warren. *A Companion to The Grapes of Wrath.* NY: Viking, 1963. Rpt NY: Penguin, 1989.

French. *Film Guide to The Grapes of Wrath.* Bloomington: Indiana U P, 1973.

*French. *JS.* NY: Twayne, rev 1975.

Garcia, Reloy. *S and D. H. Lawrence: Fictive Voices and the Ethical Imperative.* Muncie, Ind: JS Society of America, Ball State U, 1972.

Gladstein, Mimi R. *The Indestructible Women in the Works of Faulkner, Hemingway, and S.* Ann Arbor, Mich: UMI, 1986.

Gray, James. *JS.* Minneapolis: U Minnesota P, 1971.

Hayashi, Tetsumaro. *JS and the Vietnam War (Pt I).* Muncie, Ind: S Research Institute, Ball State U, 1988.

Levant, Howard. *The Novels of JS: A Critical Study.* Columbia: U Missouri P, 1974.

*Lisca, Peter. *The Wide World of JS.* New Brunswick, NJ: Rutgers U P, 1958.

*Lisca. *JS: Nature and Myth.* NY: Crowell, 1978.

Marks, Lester Jay. *Thematic Design in the Novels of JS.* The Hague: Mouton, 1969.

McCarthy, Paul. *JS.* NY: Ungar, 1980.

*Millichap, Joseph R. *S and Film.* NY: Ungar, 1983.

*Owens, Louis. *JS's Re-Vision of America.* Athens: U Georgia P, 1985.

*Owens. *The Grapes of Wrath: Trouble in the Promised Land.* Boston: Twayne, 1989.

Simmonds, Roy S. *S's Literary Achievement.* Muncie, Ind: JS Society of America, Ball State U, 1976.

*Timmerman, John H. *JS's Fiction: The Aesthetics of the Road Taken.* Norman: U Oklahoma P, 1986.

*Timmerman. *The Dramatic Landscape of S's Short Stories.* Norman: U Oklahoma P, 1990.

Watt, F W. *JS.* NY: Grove, 1962.

COLLECTIONS OF ESSAYS

*Astro, Richard & Tetsumaro Hayashi, eds. *S: The Man and His Work.* Corvallis: Oregon State U P, 1971.

*Benson, Jackson J, ed. *The Short Novels of JS: Critical Essays With a Checklist to S Criticism.* Durham, NC: Duke U P, 1990.

Bloom, Harold, ed. *Modern Critical Views: JS.* NY: Chelsea House, 1987.

Bloom, ed. *Modern Critical Views: JS's The Grapes of Wrath.* NY: Chelsea House, 1988.

Davis, Robert Con, ed. *Twentieth Century Interpretations: The Grapes of Wrath.* Englewood Cliffs, NJ: Prentice-Hall, 1982.

Davis, Robert Murray, ed. *S: A Collection of Critical Essays.* Englewood Cliffs, NJ: Prentice-Hall, 1972.

*Ditsky, John, ed. *Critical Essays on S's The Grapes of Wrath.* Boston: Hall, 1989.

*Donohue, Agnes McNeill, ed. *A Casebook on The Grapes of Wrath*. NY: Crowell, 1968.

Hayashi, Tetsumaro, ed. *S's Literary Dimension: A Guide to Comparative Studies*. Metuchen, NJ: Scarecrow, 1973.

Hayashi, ed. *A Study Guide to S: A Handbook to His Major Works*. Metuchen, NJ: Scarecrow, 1974.

Hayashi, ed. *S and The Arthurian Theme*. Muncie, Ind: JS Society of America, Ball State U, 1975.

Hayashi, ed. *A Study Guide to S's The Long Valley*. Ann Arbor, Mich: Pierian, 1976.

Hayashi, ed. *A Study Guide to S, Part II*. Metuchen, NJ: Scarecrow, 1979.

Hayashi, ed. *S's Travel Literature: Essays in Criticism*. Muncie, Ind: S Society of America, Ball State U, 1980.

Hayashi, ed. *S's The Grapes of Wrath: Essays in Criticism*. Muncie, Ind: S Research Institute, Ball State U, 1990.

Hayashi, ed. *S's Literary Dimension: A Guide to Comparative Studies, Series II*. Metuchen, NJ: Scarecrow, 1991.

Hayashi, ed. *S's Short Stories in The Long Valley: Essays in Criticism*. Muncie, Ind: S Research Institute, Ball State U, 1991.

Hayashi & Kenneth D Swan, eds. *S's Prophetic Vision of America*. Upland, Ind: Taylor U for the JS Society of America, 1976.

Hayashi & Richard F Peterson, eds. *S's Women: Essays in Criticism*. Muncie, Ind: S Society of America, Ball State U, 1979.

Hayashi & Thomas J Moore, eds. *S's The Red Pony: Essays in Criticism*. Muncie, Ind: S Research Institute, Ball State U, 1988.

Hayashi & Moore, eds. *S's Posthumous Work: Essays in Criticism*. Muncie, Ind: S Research Institute, Ball State U, 1989.

Hayashi & Yasuo Hashiguchi & Richard F Peterson, eds. *JS: East and West*. Muncie, Ind: S Society of America, Ball State U, 1978.

*Lewis, Cliff & Carroll Britch. *Rediscovering S: Revisionist Views of His Art, Politics and Intellect*. Lewiston, NY: Mellen, 1989.

Tedlock, E W & C V Wicker, eds. *S and His Critics: A Record of Twenty-five Years*. Albuquerque: U New Mexico P, 1957.

*Wyatt, David, ed. *New Essays on The Grapes of Wrath*. Cambridge: Cambridge U P, 1990.

SPECIAL JOURNALS

American Examiner, 6 (Fall–Winter 1978–1979). JS issue.

Modern Fiction Studies, 11 (Spring 1965). JS issue.

San Jose Studies, 1 (Nov 1975). JS issue.

San Jose Studies, 11 (Winter 1985). JS issue.

San Jose Studies, 16 (Winter 1990). JS issue.

San Jose Studies, 18 (Winter 1992). JS issue.

Steinbeck Quarterly (1968–).

University of Windsor Review, 8 (Spring 1973). JS issue.

BOOK SECTIONS

Allen, Mary. "The Cycle of Death, JS." *Animals in American Literature* (Urbana: U Illinois P, 1983), 115–134.

Astro, Richard. "Phlebas Sails the Caribbean: S, Hemingway, and the American Waste Land." *The Twenties,* ed Warren French (De Land, Fla: Everett/Edwards, 1975), 215–233. Rpt Hayashi, *S's Literary Dimension* (1991).

Bluestone, George. "The Grapes of Wrath." *Novels into Film* (Baltimore, Md: Johns Hopkins U P, 1957), 147–169. Rpt Davis (1972).

Cook, Sylvia Jenkins. "S's Retreat into Artfulness," "The Transformation of the Poor White in the Depression." *From Tobacco Road to Route 66* (Chapel Hill: U North Carolina P, 1976), 159–183, 184–188, 194–195.

Covici, Pascal, Jr. "From Commitment to Choice: Double Vision and the Problem of Vitality for JS." *The Fifties,* ed Warren French (De Land, Fla: Everett/Edwards, 1970), 63–71.

DeMott, Robert. "S and the Creative Process: First Manifesto to End the Bringdown Against *Sweet Thursday.*" Astro & Hayashi, 157–178.

French, Warren. "JS: A Usable Concept of Naturalism." *American Literary Naturalism: A Reassessment,* eds Yoshinobu Hakutani & Lewis Fried (Heidelberg: Winter, 1975), 122–135. Rpt Bloom (1987).

French. "JS and Modernism (A Speculation on His Contribution to the Development of the Twentieth-Century American Sensibility)." Hayashi & Swan, 35–55. Rpt Ditsky (1989).

Gladstein, Mimi R. "Female Characters in S: Minor Characters of Major Importance?" Hayashi & Peterson (1979), 17–25.

Hedgpeth, Joel W. "Philosophy on Cannery Row." Astro & Hayashi, 89–129.

*Howarth, William. "The Mother of Literature: Journalism and *The Grapes of Wrath.*" *Literary Journalism in the Twentieth Century,* ed Norman Sims (Oxford: Oxford UP, 1990), 53–81.

Kinney, Arthur F. "Tortilla Flat Re-visited." Hayashi (1975), 12–24. Rpt Bloom (1987).

Lewis, R W B. "JS: The Fitful Daemon." *The Young Rebel in American Literature,* ed Carl Bode (NY: Praeger, 1960), 119–141. Rpt *Modern American Fiction: Essays in Criticism,* ed A Walton Litz (NY: Oxford U P, 1963). Rpt Davis (1972).

Mitgang, Herbert. "The Nobel Laureates." *Dangerous Dossiers: Exposing the Secret War Against America's Greatest Authors* (NY: Fine, 1988), 71–79.

Murray, Edward. "JS, Point of View and Film." *The Cinematic Imagination* (NY: Ungar, 1972), 261–277.

*Owens, Louis. "The Mirror and the Vamp: Invention, Reflection, and Bad, Bad Cathy Trask in *East of Eden.*" *Writing the American Classics,* ed James Barbour & Tom Quirk (Chapel Hill: U North Carolina P, 1990), 235–257.

Pearson, Michael. "A Strip Angled Against the Pacific: S's California." *Imagined Places: Journeys into Literary America* (Jackson: U P Mississippi, 1991), 215–263.

*Peeler, David. *Hope Among Us Yet: Social Criticism and Social Solace in Depression America* (Athens: U Georgia P, 1987), 156–165.

*Quinones, Ricardo J. "The New American Cain: *East of Eden* and Other Works of Post–World War II America." *The Changes of Cain: Violence and the Lost Brother in Cain and Abel Literature* (Princeton, NJ: Princeton U P, 1991), 135–144.

Salter, Christopher L. "JS's *The Grapes of Wrath* as a Primer for Cultural Geography." *Humanistic Geography and Literature,* ed Douglas C D Pocock (London: Helm, 1981), 142–158. Rpt Ditsky (1989).

Shloss, Carol. "JS and Dorothea Lange: The Surveillance of Dissent." *In Visible Light: Photography and the American Writer, 1840–1940* (NY: Oxford U P, 1987), 200–231, 283–285.

Turner, Frederick. "The Valley of the World: JS's *East of Eden.*" *Spirit of Place: The Making of an American Literary Landscape* (San Francisco: Sierra Club, 1989), 247–282.

Van Antwerp, Margaret A, ed. "JS." *Dictionary of Literary Biography Documentary Series,* Vol 2 (Detroit: Bruccoli Clark/Gale, 1982), 279–332.

Wilson, Edmund. "JS." *The Boys in the Back Room* (San Francisco: Colt, 1941), 41–53. Rpt *Classics and Commercials* by Wilson (NY: Farrar, Straus, 1950).

*Wyatt, David, "S's Lost Gardens." *The Fall Into Eden* (NY: Cambridge U P, 1986), 124–157.

ARTICLES

Alexander, Stanley. "*Cannery Row:* Steinbeck's Pastoral Poem." *Western American Literature,* 2 (Winter 1968), 281–295. Rpt Davis (1972).

Astro, Richard. "S's Post-War Trilogy: A Return to Nature and the Natural Man." *Twentieth Century Literature,* 16 (Apr 1970), 109–122.

Astro. "Travels With S: The Laws of Thought and the Laws of Things." *Steinbeck Quarterly,* 8 (Spring 1975), 35–44.

Bedford, Richard C. "The Genesis and Consolation of Our Discontent." *Criticism,* 14 (Summer 1972), 277–294.

Benson, Jackson J. "'To Tom, Who Lived It': JS and the Man From Weedpatch," ". . . An Afterword and an Introduction." *Journal of Modern Literature,* 5 (Apr 1976), 151–210.

*Benson. "JS: Novelist as Scientist." *Novel,* 10 (Spring 1977), 248–264. Rpt Bloom (1987).

*Benson. "JS's *Cannery Row:* A Reconsideration." *Western American Literature,* 12 (Spring 1977), 11–40. Rpt Hayashi, *S's Literary Dimension* (1991).

*Benson. "Hemingway the Hunter and S the Farmer." *Michigan Quarterly Review,* 24 (Summer 1985), 440–460. Rpt Hayashi, *S's Literary Dimension* (1991).

*Benson & Anne Loftis. "JS and Farm Labor Unionization: The Background of *In Dubious Battle.*" *American Literature,* 52 (May 1980), 194–223.

*Britch, Carroll & Cliff Lewis. "Shadow of *The* Indian in the Fiction of JS." *MELUS,* 11 (Summer 1984), 39–58. Rev Lewis & Britch.

Burningham, Bradd. "Relation, Vision, and Tracking the Welsh Rats in *East of Eden* and *The Winter of Our Discontent.*" *Steinbeck Quarterly,* 15 (Summer–Fall 1982), 77–90.

Carlson, Eric W. "Symbolism in *The Grapes of Wrath.*" *College English,* 19 (Jan 1958), 172–175. Rpt Donohue. Rpt *The Grapes of Wrath: Text and Criticism.*

*Carpenter, Frederic I. "The Philosophical Joads." *College English,* 2 (Jan 1941), 315–325. Rpt Tedlock & Wicker. Rpt Donohue. Rpt *The Grapes of Wrath: Text and Criticism.* Rpt Bloom (1988).

Carpenter. "JS: American Dreamer." *Southwest Review,* 26 (Summer 1941), 454–467. Rpt Tedlock & Wicker.

Crockett, H Kelly. "The Bible and *The Grapes of Wrath.*" *College English,* 24 (Dec 1962), 193–199. Rpt Donohue.

Davidson, Richard A. "Hemingway, S, and the Art of the Short Story." *Steinbeck Quarterly,* 21 (Summer–Fall 1988), 73–84. Rpt Hayashi, *S's Literary Dimension* (1991).

DeMott, Robert. "The Interior Distances of JS." *Steinbeck Quarterly,* 12 (Summer–Fall 1979), 86–99.

Dewey, Joseph. "'There Was a Seedy Grandeur About the Man': Rebirth and Recovery in *Travels With Charley.*" *Steinbeck Quarterly,* 24 (Winter–Spring 1991), 22–30.

Ditsky, John M. "Music From a Dark Cave: Organic Form in S's Fiction." *Journal of Narrative Technique,* 1 (Jan 1971), 59–67.

*Eisinger, Chester E. "Jeffersonian Agrarianism in *The Grapes of Wrath.*" *University of Kansas City Review,* 14 (Winter 1947), 149–154. Rpt Donohue. Rpt *The Grapes of Wrath: Text and Criticism.*

*Everest, Beth & Judy Wedeles. "The Neglected Rib: Women in *East of Eden.*" *Steinbeck Quarterly,* 21 (Winter–Spring 1988), 13–23.

Goldhurst, William. "*Of Mice and Men:* JS's Parable of the Curse of Cain." *Western American Literature,* 6 (Summer 1971), 123–135. Rpt Benson (1990).

Govoni, Mark W. "'Symbols for the Wordlessness': The Original Manuscript of *East of Eden.*" *Steinbeck Quarterly,* 14 (Winter–Spring 1981), 14–23.

Griffin, Robert J & William A Freedman. "Machines and Animals: Pervasive Motifs in *The Grapes of Wrath.*" *Journal of English and Germanic Philology,* 62 (Jul 1963), 569–580. Rpt Donohue. Rpt *The Grapes of Wrath: Text and Criticism.*

Hayashi, Tetsumaro. "*The Pearl* as the Novel of Disengagement." *Steinbeck Quarterly,* 7 (Summer–Fall 1974), 84–88.

Jones, Lawrence W. "'A Little Play in Your Head': Parable Form in JS's Post War Fiction." *Genre,* 3 (Mar 1970), 55–63.

Levant, Howard. "*Tortilla Flat:* The Shape of JS's Career." *PMLA,* 85 (Oct 1970), 1087–1095.

Levant. "JS's *The Red Pony:* A Study in Narrative Technique." *Journal of Narrative Technique,* 1 (May 1971), 77–85. Rpt Benson (1990).

*Lieber, Todd M. "Talismanic Patterns in the Novels of JS." *American Literature,* 44 (May 1972), 262–275.

*Lisca, Peter. "*The Grapes of Wrath* as Fiction." *PMLA,* 72 (Mar 1957), 296–309. Rpt *The Modern American Novel: Essays in Criticism,* ed Max Westbrook (NY: Random House, 1966). Rpt Donohue. Rpt *The Grapes of Wrath: Text and Criticism.*

Marovitz, Sanford E. "The Expository Prose of JS (Part I)." *Steinbeck Quarterly,* 7 (Spring 1974), 41–53.

Marovitz. "The Expository Prose of JS (Part II)." *Steinbeck Quarterly,* 7 (Summer–Fall 1974), 88–102.

Metzger, Charles R. "S's Version of the Pastoral." *Modern Fiction Studies,* 6 (Summer 1960), 115–124. Rpt Benson (1990).

*Mitchell, Marilyn. "S's Strong Women: Feminine Identity in the Short Stories." *Southwest Review,* 61 (Summer 1976), 304–315. Rpt Hayashi & Peterson (1979). Rpt Bloom (1987).

Mitchell, Robin C. "S and Malory: A Correspondence With Eugene Vinaver." *Steinbeck Quarterly,* 10 (Summer–Fall 1977), 70–79.

*Mizener, Arthur. "Does a Moral Vision of the Thirties Deserve a Nobel Prize?" *New York Times Book Review* (9 Dec 1962), 4, 43–45. Rpt Donohue.

Morris, Harry. "*The Pearl:* Realism and Allegory." *English Journal,* 52 (Oct 1963), 487–495, 505. Rpt Davis (1972).

Morsberger, Robert E. "*East of Eden* on Film." *Steinbeck Quarterly,* 25 (Winter–Spring 1992), 28–42.

Mortlock, Melanie. "The Eden Myth as Paradox: An Allegorical Reading of *The Pastures of Heaven.*" *Steinbeck Quarterly,* 11 (Winter 1978), 6–15.

Motley, Warren. "From Patriarchy to Matriarchy: Ma Joad's Role in *The Grapes of Wrath.*" *American Literature,* 54 (Oct 1982), 397–412.

*Owens, Louis. "JS's 'Mystical Outcrying': *To a God Unknown* and *The Log From the Sea of Cortez.*" *San Jose Studies,* 5 (May 1979), 20–32.

*Perez, Betty L. "The Form of the Narrative Section of *Sea of Cortez:* A Specimen Collected From Reality." *Steinbeck Quarterly,* 9 (Spring 1976), 36–44. Rpt Hayashi (1980). Rpt Hayashi, *S's Literary Dimension* (1991).

Railsback, Brian. "Darwin and S: The 'Older Method' and *Sea of Cortez.*" *Steinbeck Quarterly,* 23 (Winter–Spring 1990), 27–34.

Renner, Stanley. "Sexual Idealism and Violence in 'The White Quail.'" *Steinbeck Quarterly,* 17 (Summer–Fall 1984), 76–87.

Rose, Alan Henry. "S and the Complexity of the Self in *In Dubious Battle.*" *Steinbeck Quarterly,* 9 (Winter 1976), 15–19.

Ross, Woodburn O. "JS: Naturalism's Priest." *College English,* 10 (May 1949), 432–438. Rpt Tedlock & Wicker.

Sanderson, Jim. "American Romanticism in John Ford's *The Grapes of Wrath.*" *Literature/Film Quarterly,* 17, no 4 (1989), 231–244.

Simmonds, Roy S. "'Our land. . . incredibly dear and beautiful': S's *America and Americans.*" *Steinbeck Quarterly,* 8 (Summer–Fall 1975), 89–95. Rpt Hayashi (1980).

Simpson, Hassell A. "S's Anglo-Saxon 'Wonder Words' and the American Paradox." *American Literature,* 62 (Jun 1990), 310–317.

Slater, John F. "American Past and Soviet Present: The Double Consciousness of S's *A Russian Journal*." *Steinbeck Quarterly*, 8 (Summer–Fall 1975), 95–104.

*Spilka, Mark. "Of George and Lennie and Curley's Wife: Sweet Violence in S's Eden." *Modern Fiction Studies*, 20 (Summer 1974), 169–179. Rpt Benson (1990).

Sweet, Charles A, Jr. "Ms. Elisa Allen and S's 'The Chrysanthemums.'" *Modern Fiction Studies*, 20 (Summer 1974), 210–214.

Work, James C. "Coordinate Forces in 'The Leader of the People.'" *Western American Literature*, 16 (Winter 1982), 279–289.

— *Susan Shillinglaw*

ROBERT PENN WARREN
Guthrie, Ky, 24 Apr 1905–Stratton, Vt, 15 Sep 1989

Called "America's Dean of Letters," Robert Penn Warren was the first Poet Laureate of the United States. Although he is best known for his Pulitzer Prize–winning novel, *All the King's Men,* his other nine novels and one volume of short fiction have attracted increased attention in the last decade. Moreover, since 1981 scholars have examined Warren's literary canon in toto rather than by genre. The results confirm what Cleanth Brooks wrote in the early 1960s: "The poetry, the fiction, and even the critical essays of Robert Penn Warren form a highly unified and consistent body of work." Book-length studies now focus on the autobiographical elements in and the strong poetical influences on his work.

Bibliographies

*Grimshaw, James A, Jr. *RPW: A Descriptive Bibliography, 1922–1979.* Charlottesville: U P Virginia, 1981. Primary.

*Nakadate, Neil. *RPW: A Reference Guide.* Boston: Hall, 1977. Secondary.

Books

John Brown: The Making of a Martyr. NY: Payson & Clarke, 1929. Biography.

Thirty-Six Poems. NY: Alcestis, 1935.

Night Rider. Boston: Houghton Mifflin, 1939. Novel.

Eleven Poems on the Same Theme. Norfolk, Conn: New Directions, 1942.

At Heaven's Gate. NY: Harcourt, Brace, 1943. Novel.

Selected Poems, 1923–1943. NY: Harcourt, Brace, 1944.

All the King's Men. NY: Harcourt, Brace, 1946. Novel.

Blackberry Winter. Cummington, Mass: Cummington, 1946. Story.

The Circus in the Attic and Other Stories. NY: Harcourt, Brace, 1947.

World Enough and Time: A Romantic Novel. NY: Random House, 1950.

Brother to Dragons: A Tale in Verse and Voices. NY: Random House, 1953. Verse drama.

Band of Angels. NY: Random House, 1955. Novel.

Segregation: The Inner Conflict in the South. NY: Random House, 1956. Nonfiction.

Promises: Poems, 1954–1956. NY: Random House, 1957.

Selected Essays. NY: Random House, 1958.

Remember the Alamo! NY: Random House, 1958. Children's book.

How Texas Won Her Freedom: The Story of Sam Houston & the Battle of San Jacinto. San Jacinto Monument, Tex: San Jacinto Museum of History, 1959. Nonfiction.

The Cave. NY: Random House, 1959. Novel.

The Gods of Mount Olympus. NY: Random House, 1959. Children's book.

All the King's Men: A Play. NY: Random House, 1960.

You, Emperors, and Others: Poems, 1957–1960. NY: Random House, 1960.

The Legacy of the Civil War: Meditations on the Centennial. NY: Random House, 1961. Nonfiction.

Wilderness: A Tale of the Civil War. NY: Random House, 1961. Novel.

Flood: A Romance of Our Time. NY: Random House, 1964. Novel.

Who Speaks for the Negro? NY: Random House, 1965. Nonfiction.

A Plea in Mitigation: Modern Poetry and the End of an Era. Macon, Ga: Wesleyan C, 1966. Nonfiction.

Selected Poems: New and Old, 1923–1966. NY: Random House, 1966.

Incarnations: Poems, 1966–1968. NY: Random House, 1968.

Audubon: A Vision. NY: Random House, 1969. Poem.

Homage to Theodore Dreiser. NY: Random House, 1971. Nonfiction.

Meet Me in the Green Glen. NY: Random House, 1971. Novel.

Or Else—Poem/Poems, 1968–1974. NY: Random House, 1974.

Democracy and Poetry. Cambridge, Mass & London: Harvard U P, 1975. Nonfiction.

Selected Poems, 1923–1975. NY: Random House, 1976.

A Place To Come To. NY: Random House, 1977. Novel.

Now and Then: Poems, 1976–1978. NY: Random House, 1978.

Brother to Dragons: A Tale in Verse & Voices (A New Version). NY: Random House, 1979. Verse drama.

Being Here: Poetry 1977–1980. NY: Random House, 1980.

Jefferson Davis Gets His Citizenship Back. Lexington: U P Kentucky, 1980. Nonfiction.

Ballad of a Sweet Dream of Peace: A Charade for Easter. Dallas, Tex: Pressworks, 1980. Play.

Rumor Verified: Poems, 1979–1980. NY: Random House, 1981.

Chief Joseph of the Nez Perce. NY: Random House, 1983. Poem.

New and Selected Poems, 1923–1985. NY: Random House, 1985.

Portrait of a Father. Lexington: U P Kentucky, 1988. Nonfiction.

New and Selected Essays. NY: Random House, 1989.

Other

"The Briar Patch." *I'll Take My Stand: The South and the Agrarian Tradition* by Twelve Southerners (NY & London: Harper, 1930), 246–264. Essay.

An Approach to Literature, with Cleanth Brooks, Jr & John Thibaut Purser. Baton Rouge: Louisiana State U P, 1936. Textbook.

A Southern Harvest: Short Stories by Southern Writers, ed RPW. Boston: Houghton Mifflin, 1937.

Understanding Poetry, with Brooks. NY: Holt, 1938. Textbook.

Understanding Fiction, with Brooks. NY: Crofts, 1943. Textbook.

"A Poem of Pure Imagination: An Experiment in Reading." *The Rime of the Ancient Mariner* by Samuel Taylor Coleridge (NY: Reynal & Hitchcock, 1946), 59–117. Essay.

Modern Rhetoric, with Brooks. NY: Harcourt, Brace, 1949. Textbook.

Fundamentals of Good Writing: A Handbook of Modern Rhetoric, with Brooks. NY: Harcourt, Brace, 1950.

An Anthology of Stories From the Southern Review, ed RPW & Brooks. Baton Rouge: Louisiana State U P, 1953.

Short Story Masterpieces, ed RPW & Albert Erskine. NY: Dell, 1954.

Six Centuries of Great Poetry, ed RPW & Erskine. NY: Dell, 1955.

A New Southern Harvest: An Anthology, ed RPW & Erskine. NY: Bantam, 1957.

The Scope of Fiction, with Brooks. NY: Appleton-Century-Crofts, 1960. Textbook.

Faulkner: A Collection of Critical Essays, ed RPW. Englewood Cliffs, NJ: Prentice-Hall, 1966.

Randall Jarrell, 1914–1965, ed RPW, Robert Lowell & Peter Taylor. NY: Farrar, Straus & Giroux, 1967.

Selected Poems of Herman Melville, ed RPW. NY: Random House, 1970.

John Greenleaf Whittier's Poetry, ed RPW. Minneapolis: U Minnesota P, 1971.

American Literature: The Makers and the Making, with Brooks & R W B Lewis. NY: St Martin, 1973. Textbook.

Katherine Anne Porter: A Collection of Critical Essays, ed RPW. Englewood Cliffs, NJ: Prentice-Hall, 1979.

The Essential Melville, ed RPW. NY: Ecco, 1987.

Collection

A RPW Reader, ed Albert Erskine. NY: Random House, 1987.

Manuscripts & Archives

The major collections are at the Beinecke Library, Yale U; the U of Kentucky Library; the Library, Vanderbilt U; the Center for Robert Penn Warren Studies & the Library, Western Kentucky U; & the Robert Penn Warren Birthplace, Guthrie, Ky.

Biography

BOOK

*Watkins, Floyd C. *Then and Now: The Personal Past in the Poetry of RPW.* Lexington: U P Kentucky, 1982.

BOOK SECTION

Rubin, Louis D, Jr. "RPW, 1905–1989." *The Mockingbird in the Gum Tree: A Literary Gallimaufry.* (Baton Rouge: Louisiana State U P, 1991), 137–145.

ARTICLES

Brooks, Cleanth. "A Tribute to RPW." *Southern Review,* 26 (Winter 1990), 2–4.

Core, George. "Life's Bright Parenthesis: The Example of RPW." *Hudson Review*, 43 (Summer 1990), 182–191.

Davison, Peter. "Deep in the Blackness of Woods: A Farewell to RPW." *New England Monthly* (Mar 1990), 36–39.

Grimshaw, James A, Jr. "RPW: A Reminiscence." *Gettysburg Review*, 3 (Winter 1990), 207–213.

Olney, James. "On the Death and Life of RPW." *Southern Review*, 26 (Winter 1990), 13–15.

Simpson, Lewis. "RPW and the South." *Southern Review*, 26 (Winter 1990), 7–12.

Spears, Monroe K. "RPW and the Literary Life." *Gettysburg Review*, 3 (Winter 1990), 203–206.

Sullivan, Walter. "Remembering Red." *South Carolina Review*, 23 (Fall 1990), 84–86.

Interviews

BOOKS

Watkins, Floyd C & John T Hiers, eds. *RPW Talking: Interviews, 1950–1978*. NY: Random House, 1980.

*Watkins, Hiers & Mary Louise Weaks, eds. *Talking With RPW*. Athens: U Georgia P, 1990.

BOOK SECTION

Connelly, Thomas L. "Of Bookish Men and the Fugitives: A Conversation With RPW." Edgar, 95–110.

ARTICLES

*Ellison, Ralph & Eugene Walter. "The Art of Fiction XVIII: RPW." *Paris Review*, 4 (Spring 1957), 112–140. Rpt *Writers at Work [First Series]*, ed with intro by Malcolm Cowley (NY: Viking, 1958).

Farrell, David. "Reminiscences: A Conversation With RPW." *Southern Review*, 16 (Autumn 1980), 782–798.

*Farrell. "Poetry as a Way of Life: An Interview With RPW." *Georgia Review*, 36 (Summer 1982), 314–331.

Forrest, William C & Cornelius Novelli. "The Oral Roots of Literature: An Interview With RPW." *Sewanee Review,* 89 (Summer 1981), 315–331.

Watkins, Floyd C. "A Dialogue With RPW on *Brother to Dragons.*" *Southern Review,* 16 (Winter 1980), 1–17.

Wood, Edwin Thomas. "Oh Native Soil: A Talk With RPW." *Mississippi Quarterly,* 37 (Spring 1984), 179–186.

Critical Studies

BOOKS

Bohner, Charles. *RPW.* Boston: Twayne, rev 1981.

*Burt, John. *RPW and American Idealism.* New Haven, Conn: Yale U P, 1988.

*Casper, Leonard. *RPW: The Dark and Bloody Ground.* Seattle: U Washington P, 1960.

*Clark, William Bedford. *The American Vision of RPW.* Lexington: U P Kentucky, 1991.

Guttenberg, Barnett. *Web of Being: The Novels of RPW.* Nashville, Tenn: Vanderbilt U P, 1975.

*Justus, James H. *The Achievement of RPW.* Baton Rouge: Louisiana State U P, 1981.

Longley, John Lewis, Jr. *RPW.* Austin, Tex: Steck-Vaughn, 1969.

Moore, L Hugh, Jr. *RPW and History: "The Big Myth We Live."* The Hague: Mouton, 1970.

Runyon, Randolph Paul. *The Taciturn Text: The Fiction of RPW.* Columbus: Ohio State U P, 1990.

*Ruppersburg, Hugh. *RPW and the American Imagination.* Athens: U Georgia P, 1990.

Walker, Marshall. *RPW: A Vision Earned.* Edinburgh: Harris, 1979.

West, Paul. *RPW.* Minneapolis: U Minnesota P, 1964.

COLLECTIONS OF ESSAYS

*Beebe, Maurice & Leslie A Field, eds. *RPW's All the King's Men: A Critical Handbook.* Belmont, Calif: Wadsworth, 1966.

Bloom, Harold, ed. *RPW.* NY: Chelsea House, 1986.

Bloom, ed. *Modern Critical Interpretations of RPW's All the King's Men.* NY: Chelsea House, 1987.

*Chambers, Robert H, ed. *Twentieth Century Interpretations of All the King's Men.* Englewood Cliffs, NJ: Prentice-Hall, 1977.

*Clark, William Bedford, ed. *Critical Essays on RPW.* Boston: Hall, 1981.

Edgar, Walter B, ed. *A Southern Renascence Man: Views of RPW.* Baton Rouge: Louisiana State U P, 1984.

*Gray, Richard, ed. *RPW: A Collection of Critical Essays.* Englewood Cliffs, NJ: Prentice-Hall, 1980.

Grimshaw, James A, Jr, ed. *Time's Glory: Original Essays on RPW.* Conway: U Central Arkansas P, 1986.

Hart, John A, chairman. *All the King's Men: A Symposium.* Pittsburgh, Pa: Carnegie Institute of Technology, 1957.

Light, James F, ed. *The Merrill Studies in All the King's Men.* Columbus, Ohio: Merrill, 1971.

Longley, John Lewis, Jr, ed. *RPW: A Collection of Critical Essays.* NY: NYU P, 1965.

Nakadate, Neil, ed. *RPW: Critical Perspectives.* Lexington: U P Kentucky, 1981.

*Weeks, Dennis L, ed. *"To Love So Well the World": A Festschrift in Honor of RPW.* NY: Lang, 1992.

SPECIAL JOURNALS

Four Quarters, 21 (May 1972). RPW issue.

Kentucky Review, 2, no 3 (1981). RPW issue.

Modern Fiction Studies, 6 (Spring 1960). RPW issue.

South Carolina Review, 23 (Fall 1990). RPW issue.

BOOK SECTIONS

*Brooks, Cleanth. "RPW: Experience Redeemed in Knowledge." *The Hidden God* (New Haven, Conn: Yale U P, 1963), 98–127. Rpt Gray, Bloom (1986).

Brooks. "The Crisis in Culture as Reflected in Southern Literature." *The American South,* ed Louis D Rubin, Jr (Baton Rouge: Louisiana State U P, 1980), 171–189.

Clark, William Bedford. "'Secret Sharers' in W's Later Fiction." Grimshaw (1986), 65–76.

Freedman, Carl. "Power, Sexuality, and Race in *All the King's Men*." *Southern Literature and Literary Theory*, ed Jefferson Humphries (Athens: U Georgia P, 1990), 127–141.

Justus, James. "The Power of Filiation in *All the King's Men*." *Modern American Fiction: Form and Function*, ed Thomas Daniel Young (Baton Rouge: Louisiana State U P, 1989), 156–169.

*Law, Richard G. "W's *World Enough and Time*: 'Et in Arcadia Ego.'" Grimshaw (1986), 13–43.

*Longley, John Lewis, Jr. "When All Is Said and Done: W's *Flood*." Longley (1965), 169–177.

Nakadate, Neil. "Identity, Dream, and Exploration: W's Later Fiction." Nakadate (1981), 175–189.

Olney, James. "Parents and Children in RPW's Autobiography." *Home Ground: Southern Autobiography*, ed J Bill Berry (Columbia: U Missouri P, 1991), 31–47.

*Simpson, Lewis P. *The Possibilities of Order: Cleanth Brooks and His Work* (Baton Rouge: Louisiana State U P, 1976), 1–124.

Stewart, John L. *The Burden of Time: The Fugitives and Agrarians, the Nashville Groups of the 1920's and 1930's, and the Writing of John Crowe Ransom, Allen Tate, and RPW* (Princeton, NJ: Princeton U P, 1965), 427–542.

Westendorp, Tjebbe. "*A Place To Come To*." Gray, 125–131.

Winchell, Mark Royden. "Renaissance Men: Shakespeare's Influence on RPW." *Shakespeare and Southern Writers*, ed Philip C Kolin (Jackson: U P Mississippi, 1985), 137–158.

*Woodward, C Vann. "History in RPW's Fiction." *The Future of the Past* (NY: Oxford U P, 1989), 221–234.

ARTICLES

Baker, Joseph E. "Irony in Fiction: *All the King's Men*." *College English*, 9 (Dec 1947), 122–130. Rpt Beebe & Field.

*Beebe, Keith. "Biblical Motifs in *All the King's Men*." *Journal of Bible and Religion*, 30 (Apr 1962), 123–130.

Berner, Robert. "The Required Past: *World Enough and Time*." *Modern Fiction Studies*, 6 (Spring 1960), 55–64. Rpt Gray.

*Bonds, Diane S. "Vision and Being in *A Place To Come To*." *Southern Review*, ns 16 (Autumn 1980), 816–828.

Byrne, Clifford M. "The Philosophical Development in Four of RPW's Novels." *McNeese Review,* 9 (Winter 1957), 56–68.

Campbell, Harry Modean. "W as Philosopher in *World Enough and Time.*" *Hopkins Review,* 6 (Winter 1953), 106–116.

Casper, Leonard. "Miscegenation as Symbol: *Band of Angels.*" *Audience,* 6 (Autumn 1959), 66–74.

Casper. "Trial by Wilderness: Warren's Exemplum." *Wisconsin Studies in Contemporary Literature,* 3 (Fall 1962), 45–53. Rpt Longley (1965), Gray.

Casper. "RPW's Evergreening Glen." *Texas Quarterly,* 21 (Autumn 1978), 53–63.

*Casper. "Circle With a Center Outside: RPW's *A Place To Come To.*" *Southwest Review,* 65 (Autumn 1980), 399–410.

Clark, Marden J. "Religious Implications in the Novels of RPW." *Brigham Young University Studies,* 4 (Autumn 1961), 67–79.

Clark, William Bedford. "RPW's Love Affair With America." *Southern Review,* ns 22 (Autumn 1986), 666–679.

Clements, A L. "Theme and Reality in *At Heaven's Gate* and *All the King's Men.*" *Criticism,* 5 (Winter 1963), 27–44.

Cowley, Malcolm. "RPW, aet. 75." *Georgia Review,* 35 (Spring 1981), 7–12.

Davison, Richard Allan. "RPW's 'Dialectical Configuration' and *The Cave.*" *College Language Association Journal,* 10 (Jun 1967), 349–357.

Davison. "Physical Imagery in RPW's 'Blackberry Winter.'" *Georgia Review,* 22 (Winter 1968), 482–488.

*Donaldson, Susan V. "'Let That Anvil Ring': RPW's *The Cave* and Hawthorne's Legacy." *Southern Literary Journal,* 15 (Spring 1983), 59–75.

Douglas, Wallace W. "Drug Store Gothic: The Style of RPW." *College English,* 15 (Feb 1954), 265–272.

Ford, Thomas W. "Indian Summer and Blackberry Winter: Emily Dickinson and RPW." *Southern Review,* ns 17 (Summer 1981), 542–550.

Girault, Norton R. "The Narrator's Mind as Symbol: An Analysis of *All the King's Men.*" *Accent,* 7 (Summer 1947), 220–234. Rpt Beebe & Field, Chambers, Nakadate (1981).

Gray, Richard. "The American Novelist and American History: A Revaluation of *All the King's Men.*" *Journal of American Studies,* 6 (Dec 1972), 297–307. Rpt Bloom (1987).

Grimshaw, James A, Jr. "Strong to Stark: Deceiver, Demagogue, Dictator." *Texas College English,* 23 (Fall 1990), 17–22.

*Hardy, John Edward. "RPW's Double-Hero." *Virginia Quarterly Review,* 36 (Autumn 1960), 583–597.

Heilman, Robert B. "Melpomene as Wallflower; or, The Reading of Tragedy." *Sewanee Review,* 55 (Jan–Mar 1947), 154–166. Rpt Longley (1965), Beebe & Field, Chambers.

Heilman. "Tangled Web." *Sewanee Review,* 59 (Jan–Mar 1951), 107–119. Rpt Longley (1965), Nakadate (1981).

Herndon, Jerry A. "A Probable Source for the Buffalo-Hunting Episodes in RPW's *Night Rider.*" *Rendezvous,* 11 (Spring 1976), 53–62.

Herring, H D. "Madness in *At Heaven's Gate:* A Metaphor of the Self in W's Fiction." *Four Quarters,* 21 (May 1972), 56–66.

Johnson, Glen M. "The Pastness of *All the King's Men.*" *American Literature,* 51 (Jan 1980), 553–557.

*Jones, Madison. "The Novels of RPW." *South Atlantic Quarterly,* 62 (Autumn 1963), 488–498.

*Justus, James H. "W's *World Enough and Time* and Beauchamp's Confession." *American Literature,* 33 (Jan 1962), 500–511.

Justus. "The Politics of the Self-Created: *At Heaven's Gate.*" *Sewanee Review,* 82 (Spring 1974), 284–299. Rpt Gray.

*Justus. "Burden's Willie." *South Carolina Review,* 23 (Fall 1990), 29–35.

Katope, Christopher G. "RPW's *All the King's Men:* A Novel of 'Pure Imagination.'" *Texas Studies in Literature and Language,* 12 (Fall 1970), 493–510.

*Kehl, D G. "Love's Definition: Dream as Reality in RPW's *Meet Me in the Green Glen.*" *Four Quarters,* 21 (May 1972), 116–122.

Kerr, Elizabeth. "Polarity of Themes in *All the King's Men.*" *Modern Fiction Studies,* 6 (Spring 1960), 25–46. Rpt Beebe & Field.

Law, Richard G. "Warren's *Night Rider* and the Issue of Naturalism: The 'Nightmare' of Our Age." *Southern Literary Journal,* 8 (Spring 1976), 41–61. Rpt Nakadate (1981), Bloom (1986).

*Law. "*At Heaven's Gate:* 'The Fires of Irony.'" *American Literature,* 53 (Mar 1981), 87–104.

Longley, John Lewis, Jr. "*At Heaven's Gate:* The Major Themes." *Modern Fiction Studies,* 6 (Spring 1960), 13–24. Rpt Longley (1965).

Magaw, Malcolm O. "Pilgrimage to Ambivalence: A Reinterpretation of RPW's *A Place To Come To.*" *Midwest Quarterly,* 29 (Summer 1988), 469–486.

McDowell, Frederick P W. "The Romantic Tragedy of Self in *World Enough and Time.*" *Critique,* 1 (Summer 1957), 34–48. Rpt Longley (1965).

Meckier, Jerome. "Burden's Complaint: The Disintegrated Personality as Theme and Style in W's *All the King's Men.*" *Studies in the Novel,* 2 (Spring 1970), 7–21. Rpt Chambers.

*Nakadate, Neil. "RPW and the Confessional Novel." *Genre,* 2 (Dec 1969), 326–340.

*Newton, Thomas A. "A Character Index of RPW's Long Works of Fiction." *Emporia State Research Studies,* 26 (Winter 1978).

Payne, Ladell. "Willie Stark and Huey Long: Atmosphere, Myth, or Suggestion?" *American Quarterly,* 20 (Fall 1968), 580–595. Rpt Chambers, Nakadate (1981).

Ray, Robert J & Ann. "Time in *All the King's Men:* A Stylistic Analysis." *Texas Studies in Literature and Language,* 5 (Autumn 1963), 452–457.

*Rocks, James E. "Warren's 'Blackberry Winter': A Reading." *University of Mississippi Studies in English,* ns 1 (1980), 97–105.

*Rubin, Louis D, Jr. "All the King's Meanings." *Georgia Review,* 8 (Winter 1954), 422–434.

Ryan, Alvan S. "RPW's *Night Rider:* The Nihilism of the Isolated Temperament." *Modern Fiction Studies,* 7 (Winter 1961–1962), 338–346. Rpt Longley (1965), Gray.

*Shepherd, Allen. "Character and Theme in RPW's *Flood.*" *Critique,* 9, no 3 (1967), 95–102.

Shepherd. "RPW as a Philosophical Novelist." *Western Humanities Review,* 24 (Spring 1970), 157–168. Rpt Bloom (1987).

Shepherd. "Character and Theme in W's *Meet Me in the Green Glen.*" *Greyfriar,* 13 (1972), 34–41.

Shepherd. "Toward an Analysis of the Prose Style of RPW." *Studies in American Fiction,* 1 (Autumn 1973), 188–202. Rpt Clark.

Simmons, James C. "Adam's Lobectomy Operation and the Meaning of *All the King's Men.*" *PMLA,* 86 (Jan 1971), 84–89. Rpt Chambers.

*Simpson, Lewis P. "RPW: The Loneliness Artist." *Sewanee Review,* 99 (Summer 1991), 337–361.

Slotkin, Alan R. "The Language of Social Interactions: The Idiolect of Willie Stark in RPW's *All the King's Men.*" *College Language Association Journal,* 30 (Mar 1987), 294–306.

Strandberg, Victor. "RPW and the Search for Design." *Gettysburg Review,* 5 (Summer 1992), 480–497.

Sullivan, Walter. "The Historical Novelist and the Existential Peril: RPW's *Band of Angels.*" *Southern Literary Journal,* 2 (Spring 1970), 104–116. Rpt Nakadate (1981), Bloom (1986).

*Tucker, Kenneth. "The Pied Piper—A Key to Understanding RPW's 'Blackberry Winter.'" *Studies in Short Fiction,* 19 (Fall 1982), 339–342.

Waldrep, Christopher. "William Faulkner, RPW, and the Law." *Southern Studies,* ns 2 (Spring 1991), 39–50.

*Watkins, Floyd C. "Following the Tramp in W's 'Blackberry Winter.'" *Studies in Short Fiction,* 22 (Summer 1985), 343–345.

*Weaks, Mary Louise. "The Search for a 'Terra' in *A Place To Come To.*" *Mississippi Quarterly,* 37 (Fall 1984), 455–468.

Weathers, Winston. "'Blackberry Winter' and the Use of Archetypes." *Studies in Short Fiction,* 1 (Fall 1963), 45–51.

*Wilcox, Earl J. "'A Cause for Laughter, a Thing for Tears': Humor in *All the King's Men.*" *Southern Literary Journal,* 12 (Fall 1979), 27–35.

Wilhelm, Albert E. "Images of Initiation in RPW's 'Blackberry Winter.'" *Studies in Short Fiction,* 17 (Summer 1980), 343–345.

*Witte, Flo. "Adam's Rebirth in RPW's *Wilderness.*" *Southern Quarterly,* 12 (Jul 1974), 365–377.

— James A. Grimshaw, Jr.

THOMAS WOLFE

Asheville, NC, 3 Oct 1900–Baltimore, Md, 15 Sep 1938

Thomas Wolfe's four novels—*Look Homeward, Angel; Of Time and the River; The Web and the Rock;* and *You Can't Go Home Again*—gave expression to themes central to the American consciousness: the isolation and alienation of young manhood, the drive for sexual fulfillment and intellectual growth in a restrictive society, the triumph and education of the young artist, the search for home and father, and the obsession with death and time. Recent critics have concerned themselves with the authority of the posthumously published novels, which were heavily edited by Edward Aswell. What remains undisputed, however, is the vigor of Wolfe's prose style that, through use of repetitive structures, builds to epiphanies—moments in which the memories of the past, the realities of the present, and the promises of the future fuse in a single consciousness.

Bibliographies

*Johnston, Carol. *TW: A Descriptive Bibliography*. Pittsburgh, Pa: U Pittsburgh P, 1987. Primary.

*Phillipson, John S. *TW: A Reference Guide*. Boston: Hall, 1977. Secondary.

Phillipson. "TW: A Reference Guide Updated." *Resources for American Literary Study*, 11 (Spring 1981), 37–80. Secondary.

BOOKS

The Crisis in Industry. Chapel Hill: U North Carolina Department of Philosophy, 1919. Essay.

Look Homeward, Angel. NY: Scribners, 1929. Novel.

Of Time and the River. NY: Scribners, 1935. Novel.

From Death to Morning. NY: Scribners, 1935. Stories.

The Story of a Novel. NY & London: Scribners, 1936. Essay.

A Note on Experts: Dexter Vespasian Joyner. NY: House of Books, 1939. Story.

The Web and the Rock. NY & London: Harper, 1939. Novel.

You Can't Go Home Again. NY & London: Harper, 1940. Novel.

The Hills Beyond. NY & London: Harper, 1941. Stories.

Gentlemen of the Press. Chicago: Targ, 1942. Play.

Mannerhouse: A Play in a Prologue and Three Acts. NY: Harper, 1948. Augmented ed, *Mannerhouse: A Play in a Prologue and Four Acts by TW,* ed Louis D Rubin, Jr & John L Idol, Jr. Baton Rouge & London: Louisiana State U P, 1985.

TW's Purdue Speech: "Writing and Living," ed William Braswell & Leslie A Field. West Lafayette, Ind: Purdue U Studies, 1964.

The Mountains, ed Pat M Ryan. Chapel Hill: U North Carolina P, 1970. Play.

A Prologue to America, ed Aldo P Magi. Athens, Ohio: Croissant, 1978. Story.

Welcome to Our City, ed Richard S Kennedy. Baton Rouge & London: Louisiana State U P, 1983. Play.

K-19: Salvaged Pieces, ed Idol. Npl: TW Society, 1983. Facsimile of unfinished novel.

The Hound of Darkness, ed Idol. Npl: TW Society, 1986. Play.

The Starwick Episodes, ed Kennedy. Npl: TW Society, 1989. Deleted material from *Of Time and the River.*

The Good Child's River, ed Suzanne Stutman. Chapel Hill & London: U North Carolina P, 1991. Novel.

The Lost Boy, ed James W Clark, Jr. Chapel Hill & London: U North Carolina P, 1992. Novella.

Letters, Diaries, Notebooks

TW's Letters to His Mother, ed John Skally Terry. NY: Scribners, 1943.

. . . The Years of Wandering in Many Lands and Cities. NY: Boesen, 1949. Journal.

A Western Journal: A Daily Log of the Great Parks Trip June 20–July 2, 1938. Pittsburgh, Pa: U Pittsburg P, 1951.

The Correspondence of TW and Homer Andrew Watt, ed Oscar Cargill & Thomas Clark Pollock. NY: NYU P & London: Cumberlege/Oxford U P, 1954.

The Letters of TW, ed Elizabeth Nowell. NY: Scribners, 1956; abridged as *Selected Letters of TW.* London & c: Heinemann, 1958.

The Letters of TW to His Mother, ed C Hugh Holman & Sue Fields Ross. Chapel Hill: U North Carolina P, 1968.

The Notebooks of TW, 2 vols, ed Richard S Kennedy & Paschal Reeves. Chapel Hill: U North Carolina P, 1970.

Beyond Love and Loyalty: The Letters of TW and Elizabeth Nowell, Together With "No More Rivers," a Story by TW, ed Kennedy. Chapel Hill & London: U North Carolina P, 1983.

My Other Loneliness: Letters of TW and Aline Bernstein, ed Suzanne Stutman. Chapel Hill & London: U North Carolina P, 1983.

In the Shadow of the Giant: TW, ed Mary Aswell Doll & Clara Stites. Athens: Ohio U P, 1988. Letters.

TW's Composition Books: The North State Fitting School, 1912–1915, ed Alice R Cotten & John L Idol, Jr. Chapel Hill: North Caroliniana Society/TW Society, 1990. Notebooks.

The Autobiographical Outline for Look Homeward, Angel, ed Lucy Conniff & Kennedy. Npl: TW Society, 1991. Notebooks.

Collections

The Face of a Nation: Poetical Passages From the Writings of TW. NY: Scribners, 1939.

Stories by TW, ed Jo Meyers & E B Williams. NY: Avon, 1944.

A Stone, a Leaf, a Door: Poems by TW. NY: Scribners, 1945.

The Portable TW, ed Maxwell Geismar. NY: Viking, 1946. Repub as *The Indispensable TW*. NY: Book Society, 1950. Repub as *Selections From the Works of TW*. London & c: Heinemann, 1952.

TW Short Stories. NY: Penguin, 1947.

The Short Novels of TW, ed C Hugh Holman. NY: Scribners, 1961.

The TW Reader, ed Holman. NY: Scribners, 1962.

The Autobiography of an American Novelist, ed Leslie Field. Cambridge & London: Harvard U P, 1983. Essay & speech.

The Complete Short Stories of TW, ed Francis Skipp; foreword by James Dickey. NY: Scribners, 1987.

Manuscripts & Archives

The major collections are at the Houghton Library, Harvard U; U of North Carolina, Chapel Hill, Library; Princeton U Library; & Pack Memorial Library, Asheville, NC.

Biographies

BOOKS

Adams, Agatha Boyd. *TW: Carolina Student, a Brief Biography*. Chapel Hill: U North Carolina Library, 1950.

Berger, Brian F. *TW: The Final Journey*. West Linn, Oreg: Willamette River, 1984.

Boyd, Madeleine. *TW: The Discovery of a Genius*, ed Aldo P Magi. Npl: TW Society, 1981.

*Donald, David Herbert. *Look Homeward: A Life of TW*. Boston: Little, Brown, 1987.

Hoagland, Clayton & Kathleen. *TW, Our Friend: 1933–1938*, ed Aldo P Magi & Richard Walser. Athens, Ohio: Croissant, 1979.

Magi, Aldo P & Richard Walser. *W and Belinda Jelliffe*. Npl: TW Society, 1987.

*Nowell, Elizabeth. *TW: A Biography*. Garden City, NY: Doubleday, 1960.

Pollock, Thomas Clark & Oscar Cargill. *TW at Washington Square*. NY: NYU P, 1954.

Raynolds, Robert. *TW: Memoir of a Friendship*. Austin: U Texas P, 1965.

Turnbull, Andrew. *TW*. NY: Scribners, 1967.

Walser, Richard. *TW: Undergraduate*. Durham, NC: Duke U P, 1977.

Wheaton, Mabel Wolfe & LeGette Blythe. *TW and His Family*. Garden City, NY: Doubleday, 1961.

Wisdom, William. *The Table Talk of TW*, ed John S Phillipson. Npl: TW Society, 1988.

BOOK SECTIONS

Berg, A Scott. *Max Perkins: Editor of Genius* (NY: Dutton, 1978), passim.

Cane, Melville. "TW: A Memoir." *The First Firefly* (NY: Harcourt Brace Jovanovich, 1974), 37–49.

Klein, Carole. *Aline* (NY: Harper & Row, 1979), passim.

ARTICLES

Aswell, Edward C. "TW Did Not Kill Maxwell Perkins." *Saturday Review of Literature*, 34 (6 Oct 1951), 16–17, 44–46.

Barber, Philip W. "TW Writes a Play." *Harper's*, 216 (May 1958), 71–76.

Bishop, Don. "TW as a Student." *Carolina Magazine*, 71 (Mar 1942), 28–29, 35, 47–48.

Braswell, William. "TW Lectures and Takes a Holiday." *College English*, 1 (Oct 1939), 11–22.

Davis, Ruth. "*Look Homeward, Angel.*" *Saturday Review of Literature*, 29 (5 Jan 1946), 13–14, 31–32.

Kennedy, Richard S. "TW at Harvard, 1920–1923." *Harvard Library Bulletin*, 4 (Spring–Autumn 1950), 172–190, 304–319.

Kennedy. "TW at New York University." *Thomas Wolfe Newsletter*, 5 (Fall 1981), 1–10.

Ledig-Rowohlt, H M. "TW in Berlin." *Der Monat*, 1 (Oct 1948), 69–77.

McCoy, George W. "Asheville and TW." *North Carolina Historical Review*, 30 (Apr 1953), 200–217.

*Perkins, Maxwell. "Scribner's and TW." *Carolina Magazine*, 68 (Oct 1938), 15–17.

*Perkins. "TW." *Harvard Library Bulletin*, 1 (Autumn 1947), 269–277.

Roberts, Terry. "Paul Green Remembers TW's Funeral." *Thomas Wolfe Newsletter*, 12 (Fall 1988), 4–11.

Interviews

BOOK

TW Interviewed: 1929–1938, ed Aldo P Magi & Richard Walser. Baton Rouge: Louisiana State U P, 1985.

Critical Studies

BOOKS

Field, Leslie A. *TW and His Editors: Establishing a True Text for the Posthumous Publications*. Norman: U Oklahoma P, 1987.

Gurko, Leo. *TW: Beyond the Romantic Ego*. NY: Crowell, 1975.

*Holman, C Hugh. *TW*. Minneapolis: U Minnesota P, 1960.

Holman. *The Loneliness at the Core: Studies in TW*. Baton Rouge: Louisiana State U P, 1975.

*Idol, John Lane, Jr. *A TW Companion*. Westport, Conn: Greenwood, 1987.

Johnson, Pamela Hansford. *TW: A Critical Study*. London: Heinemann, 1947; *Hungry Gulliver: An English Critical Appraisal of TW*. NY: Scribners, 1948. Repub as *The Art of TW*. NY: Scribners, 1963.

*Kennedy, Richard S. *The Window of Memory: The Literary Career of TW*. Chapel Hill: U North Carolina P, 1962.

Muller, Herbert J. *TW*. Norfolk, Conn: New Directions, 1947.

Reeves, Paschal. *TW's Albatross: Race and Nationality in America*. Athens: U Georgia P, 1968.

*Rubin, Louis D, Jr. *TW: The Weather of His Youth*. Baton Rouge: Louisiana State U P, 1955.

Snyder, William U. *TW: Ulysses and Narcissus*. Athens: Ohio U P, 1971.

Walser, Richard. *TW: An Introduction and Interpretation*. NY: Barnes & Noble, 1961.

Watkins, Floyd C. *TW's Characters: Portraits From Life*. Norman: U Oklahoma P, 1957.

COLLECTIONS OF ESSAYS

Bloom, Harold, ed. *TW*. NY: Chelsea House, 1987.

*Field, Leslie A, ed. *TW: Three Decades of Criticism*. NY: NYU P, 1968.

*Holman, C Hugh, ed. *The World of TW*. NY: Scribners, 1962.

Jones, H G, ed. *TW of North Carolina*. Chapel Hill: North Caroliniana Society & North Carolina Collection, 1982.

Jones, ed. *TW at Eighty-Seven*. Chapel Hill: North Caroliniana Society & North Carolina Collection, 1988.

Kennedy, Richard S, ed. *TW: A Harvard Perspective*. Athens, Ohio: Croissant, 1983.

*Phillipson, John S, ed. *Critical Essays on TW*. Boston: Hall, 1985.

Reeves, Paschal, ed. *TW and the Glass of Time*. Athens: U Georgia P, 1971.

*Reeves, ed. *TW: The Critical Reception*. NY: Lewis, 1974.

Rubin, Louis D, Jr, ed. *TW: A Collection of Critical Essays*. Englewood Cliffs, NJ: Prentice-Hall, 1973.

*Walser, Richard S, ed. *The Enigma of TW: Biographical and Critical Selections*. Cambridge: Harvard U P, 1953.

SPECIAL JOURNALS

Carolina Magazine, 68 (Oct 1938). TW issue.

Thomas Wolfe Newsletter (1977–1981).

Thomas Wolfe Review (1981–). Includes checklists.

BOOK SECTIONS

Aswell, Edward C. "A Note on TW." *The Hills Beyond* (NY: Harper, 1941), 349–386.

Clark, James W, Jr. "'The Lost Boy' and the Line of Life." Jones (1988), 61–70.

Hagan, John. "TW's *Of Time and the River:* The Quest for Transcendence." Kennedy (1983), 3–20.

Johnston, Carol. "TW: Detailing a Literary Career." Jones (1988), 9–19.

Van Antwerp, Margaret A, ed. "TW." *Dictionary of Literary Biography Documentary Series,* Vol 2 (Detroit: Bruccoli Clark/Gale, 1982), 333–396.

Walser, Richard. "The Angel and the Ghost." Reeves (1971), 45–77.

ARTICLES

Albrecht, W P. "The Titles of *Look Homeward, Angel: A Story of the Buried Life.*" *Modern Language Quarterly,* 11 (Mar 1950), 50–57.

Bassett, John E. "*Of Time and the River:* Critics and Reviewers." *University of Mississippi Studies in English,* ns 9 (1991), 26–41.

Boyer, James D. "A Reevaluation of W's 'Only the Dead Know Brooklyn.'" *South Carolina Review,* 20 (Fall 1987), 45–49.

De Voto, Bernard. "Genius Is Not Enough." *Saturday Review of Literature,* 13 (25 Apr 1936), 3–4, 14.

Domnarski, William. "TW's Success as Short Novelist: Structure and Theme in *A Portrait of Bascom Hawke.*" *Southern Literary Journal,* 13 (Fall 1980), 32–41.

Donald, David Herbert. "Look Homeward: TW and the South." *Southern Review,* 23 (Apr 1987), 241–255.

Donald. "An Author and His Editor: TW and Maxwell Perkins." *Chadakoin Review,* 1 (Summer 1988), 39–53.

Field, Leslie A. "A 'True Text' Experience: TW and Posthumous Publication." *Thomas Wolfe Newsletter,* 6 (Fall 1982), 27–34.

Foster, Ruel E. "TW's Mountain Gloom and Glory." *American Literature,* 44 (Jan 1973), 638–647.

Green, Charmian. "W's Stonecutter Once Again: An Unpublished Episode." *Mississippi Quarterly,* 30 (Fall 1977), 611–623.

Hagan, John. "Structure, Theme, and Metaphor in TW's *Look Homeward, Angel.*" *American Literature,* 53 (May 1981), 266–285.

Hagan. "'The Whole Passionate Enigma of Life': TW on Nature and the Youthful Quest." *Thomas Wolfe Newsletter,* 7 (Spring 1983), 32–42.

Halberstadt, John. "The Making of TW's Posthumous Novels." *Yale Review,* ns 70 (Oct 1980), 79–94.

Halberstadt, "The 'Creative Editing' of TW." *Harvard Magazine,* 84 (Jan–Feb 1982), 41–42, 44–46.

*Holman, C Hugh. "TW and the Stigma of Autobiography." *Virginia Quarterly Review*, 40 (Autumn 1964), 614–625.

*Holman. "TW and America." *Southern Literary Journal*, 10 (Fall 1977), 56–74.

Idol, John L, Jr. "The Plays of TW and Their Links With His Novels." *Mississippi Quarterly*, 22 (Spring 1969), 95–112.

Idol. "TW and Jonathan Swift." *South Carolina Review*, 8 (Nov 1975), 43–54.

Idol. "Angels and Demons: The Satire of *Look Homeward, Angel.*" *Studies in Contemporary Satire*, 1 (1976), 39–46.

Idol. "Responses of Contemporary Novelists to *Look Homeward, Angel.*" *Thomas Wolfe Newsletter*, 3 (Fall 1979), 2–8.

Idol. "TW and T. S. Eliot: The Hippopotamus and the Old Possum." *Southern Literary Journal*, 13 (Spring 1981), 15–26.

Idol. "Ernest Hemingway and TW." *South Carolina Review*, 15 (Fall 1982), 24–31.

Johnston, Carol. "The Critical Reception of *Of Time and the River.*" *Thomas Wolfe Newsletter*, 11 (Spring 1987), 45–54.

*Kennedy, Richard S. "W's *Look Homeward, Angel* as a Novel of Development." *South Atlantic Quarterly*, 63 (Spring 1964), 218–226.

Kennedy. "TW and the American Experience." *Modern Fiction Studies*, 11 (Autumn 1965), 219–233.

Kennedy. "TW's Last Manuscript." *Harvard Library Bulletin*, 23 (Apr 1975), 203–211.

Kennedy. "The 'Wolfegate' Affair." *Harvard Magazine*, 84 (Sep–Oct 1981), 48–53, 62.

Kennedy. "W's *Look Homeward, Angel* in the Literary Marketplace." *Thomas Wolfe Newsletter*, 6 (Fall 1982), 23–26.

Kennedy. "What the Galley Proofs of W's *Of Time and the River* Tell Us." *Thomas Wolfe Newsletter*, 9 (Fall 1985), 1–8.

"The Last Letter of TW, and the Reply to It." *Harvard Library Bulletin*, 1 (Autumn 1947), 278–279.

Miehe, Patrick. "The Outline of TW's Last Book." *Harvard Library Bulletin*, 21 (Oct 1973), 400–401.

Millichap, Joseph R. "Narrative Structure and Symbolic Imagery in *Look Homeward, Angel.*" *Southern Humanities Review*, 7 (Summer 1973), 295–303.

O'Brien, Daphne H. "'The Banquet of Life': Hunger and Plenty in *Look Homeward, Angel.*" *Thomas Wolfe Newsletter*, 12 (Fall 1988), 23–32.

Owen, Guy. "'An Angel on the Porch' and *Look Homeward, Angel.*" *Thomas Wolfe Newsletter,* 4 (Fall 1980), 21–24.

Pusey, William W, III. "The German Vogue of TW." *Germanic Review,* 23 (Apr 1948), 131–148.

Reaver, J Russell & Robert I Strozier. "TW and Death." *Georgia Review,* 16 (Fall 1962), 330–350.

Rubin, Louis D, Jr. "TW and the Place He Came From." *Virginia Quarterly Review,* 52 (Spring 1976), 183–202.

Skipp, Francis E. "The Editing of *Look Homeward, Angel.*" *Papers of the Bibliographical Society of America,* 57 (First Quarter 1963), 1–13.

Skipp. "*Of Time and the River:* The Final Editing." *Papers of the Bibliographical Society of America,* 64 (Third Quarter 1970), 313–322.

*Warren, Robert Penn. "A Note on the Hamlet of TW." *American Review,* 5 (May 1935), 191–208.

Whitlow, Karen L. "TW and the 'Incommunicable' Prison." *Thomas Wolfe Newsletter,* 12 (Fall 1988), 38–49.

— *Carol Johnston*
This entry has been revised and updated by the series editors.

A CHECKLIST FOR STUDENTS
OF AMERICAN FICTION

Sixty-eight works and five periodicals essential to the study of modern American fiction.

These reference sources are intended to aid research on general aspects of American literature and its connections with other fields. Tools specific to genres, periods, and authors are listed under those rubrics in the appropriate *Essential Bibliography of American Fiction* volumes.

Historical Background

1. *American Studies: An Annotated Bibliography,* ed Jack Salzman. Cambridge: Cambridge U P, 1986. 3 vols. Supplement, 1990.
   Summaries of books on U.S. society & culture; well-organized, useful index.
2. *Dictionary of American Biography,* ed Allen Johnson, Dumas Malone et al. NY: Scribners, 1928– . 20 vols, 8 supplements & index.
   Generally excellent scholarly essays with brief bibliographies.
3. *Dictionary of American History,* ed Louise B Katz. NY: Scribners, 1976–1978. 7 vols & index.
   Careful identification of events, places & movements. For biographies, use *DAB* (#2).
4. *Encyclopedia of American Facts and Dates* by Gorton Carruth. 8th ed, NY: Harper & Row, 1987.
   Best chronology of American history.
5. *Guide to the Study of the United States of America: Representative Books Reflecting the Development of American Life and Thought,* ed Roy P Basler et al. Washington: Library of Congress, 1960. Supplement, 1976.
   Annotated list of titles.
6. *Harvard Guide to American History,* ed Frank Freidel. Cambridge: Harvard U P, rev 1974. 2 vols.
   Selective topical bibliographies.
7. *Oxford Companion to American History,* ed Thomas H Johnson. NY: Oxford U P, 1966.

8. *Oxford History of the American People* by Samuel Eliot Morison. NY: Oxford U P, 1965.

The American Language

9. *The American Language: An Inquiry into the Development of English in the United States* by H L Mencken. 4th ed, NY: Knopf, 1936. Supplements, 1945 & 1948.
   Personalized narrative on history & quirks of written & spoken American English.
10. *Dictionary of American English on Historical Principles,* ed William A Craigie & James R Hulbert. Chicago: U Chicago P, 1938–1944. 4 vols.
    American complement to *OED* (# 12).
11. *New Dictionary of American Slang,* ed Robert L Chapman. NY: Harper & Row, 1986.
12. *Oxford English Dictionary.* 2nd ed, ed J A Simpson & E S C Weiner, Oxford: Oxford U P, 1989. 20 vols.†
    An historical dictionary, chronicling meanings & usage of 500,000 words over a millenium. Heavily British, so balanced by Craigie & Hulbert (# 10).

Literature

QUOTATIONS

13. *Familiar Quotations: A Collection of Passages, Phrases, and Proverbs Traced to Their Sources in Ancient and Modern Literature* by John Bartlett. 16th ed, ed Justin Kaplan et al, Boston: Little, Brown, 1992.
    Standard, updated compilation, arranged by author & date; well-indexed.
14. *A New Dictionary of Quotations on Historical Principles From Ancient and Modern Sources* by H L Mencken. NY: Knopf, 1942.
    Among the many books of quotations, this may rank highest for literary interest.

---

† Daggers indicate works that are at least partly available by computer. See note on "Computer Availability" at the end of this checklist

LITERARY HISTORIES

15. *Annals of American Literature 1602–1983*, ed Richard M Ludwig & Clifford A Nault, Jr. NY: Oxford U P, 1986.
    Chronology of significant literary events & publications.
16. *Cambridge History of American Literature,* ed William Peterfield Trent et al. Cambridge: Cambridge U P / NY: Putnam, 1917–1921. 4 vols.
    Exhaustive treatment for 17th through 19th centuries.
17. *Literary History of the United States: History.* 4th ed, ed Robert E Spiller et al. NY: Macmillan / London: Collier Macmillan, 1974.
    Particularly strong for pre-World War I literature & background. See # 45.

LITERARY DICTIONARIES

18. *Benét's Reader's Encyclopedia of American Literature,* ed George Perkins, Barbara Perkins & Philip Leininger. NY: Harper Collins, 1991.
    Lively discussion of authors, terms & historical allusions.
19. *A Handbook to Literature* by C Hugh Holman. 6th ed, NY: Macmillan, 1992.
    Essential dictionary of literary terminology. Comprehensive, with useful appendixes.
20. *Oxford Companion to American Literature.* 5th ed, ed James D Hart. NY: Oxford U P, 1983.
    Oxford Companions are standards of pithy identifications of authors, works, characters in literature & may also contain useful appendixes.

LITERARY BIOGRAPHIES

21. *American Women Writers: A Critical Reference Guide From Colonial Times to the Present,* ed Lina Mainiero. NY: Ungar, 1979–1982. 4 vols.
    Critical biography & selected bibliography for 1,000 writers, many not covered elsewhere.
22. *American Writers.* NY: Scribners, 1974. 4 vols. 2-vol supplements, 1979, 1981, 1991.
    Scholarly essays with selective bibliographies. Based on the *U Minnesota Pamphlets on American Writers.*
23. *Black American Writers, Past and Present: A Biographical and Bibliographical Dictionary,* ed Theressa Gunnels Rush et al. Metuchen, NJ: Scarecrow, 1975.
    Uneven guide to 2,000 writers.

24. *Contemporary Authors: A Bio-Bibliographical Guide to Current Writers in Fiction, General Nonfiction, Poetry, Journalism, Drama, Motion Pictures, Television, and Other Fields.* Detroit: Gale, 1962– .160 vols to date. †

    Biographical, occasionally critical information, regularly revised, very current. *Bibliographic Series,* 2 volumes to date, provides extensive bibliographies on authors.

25. *Dictionary of Literary Biography.* Detroit: Bruccoli Clark Layman/Gale, 1978– . 162 vols to date.

    Scholarly, illustrated, critical-biographical essays with bibliographies. Individual volumes cover international literatures by nationality, genre & period. Includes *Yearbooks* and *Documentary Series* volumes. Also *Concise Dictionary of American Literary Biography,* 1987–1989, 6 vols. Cumulatively indexed.

26. *Twentieth Century Authors,* ed Stanley J Kunitz & Howard Haycraft. NY: Wilson, 1942. Supplement, ed Kunitz & Vineta Colby, 1955.

27. *World Authors, 1950–1970,* ed John Wakeman. NY: Wilson, 1975. Supplements, *1970–1975* (1980); *1975–1980,* ed Vineta Colby (1985); *1980–1985,* ed Colby (1991).

PRIMARY BIBLIOGRAPHIES

28. *Bibliography of American Literature,* ed Jacob Blanck. New Haven, Conn: Yale U P, 1955–1991. 9 vols.

    Primary bibliographies of books by nearly 300 authors who died before 1931.

29. *Books in Print.* NY: Bowker, 1948– . Annually with updates.

    Listing by author, title & subject of books available from or projected by major American publishers.

30. *Cumulative Book Index.* NY: Wilson, 1933– . Quarterly, cumulated annually. †

    English language books published internationally. See #37.

31. *First Printings of American Authors: Contributions Toward Descriptive Checklists.* Detroit: Bruccoli Clark/Gale, 1977–1987. 5 vols.

    Listings for many authors not found elsewhere.

32. *Facts On File Bibliography of American Fiction: 1919–1988,* 2 vols, ed Matthew J Bruccoli & Judith S Baughman; *1866–1918,* 1 vol, ed James Nagel & Gwen L Nagel; *1588–1865,* 1 vol, ed Kent P Ljungquist. NY: Manly/Facts On File, 1991–1993.

    Listing of books by & selected criticism of authors between 1588 and 1988.

33. *National Union Catalog, Pre-1956 Imprints.* London: Mansell, 1968–1980. 685 vols. Supplementary vols 686–754.

Listing by author of all books published before 1956 & owned by American research libraries, including the Library of Congress. Basic bibliographical information with locations.

34. *National Union Catalog, 1956–1967,* 125 vols, Totowa, NJ: Rowman & Littlefield, 1972; *1968–1972,* 104 vols, Ann Arbor, Mich: Edwards, 1973; *1973–1977,* 135 vols, Totowa, NJ: Rowman & Littlefield, 1978. Annual, *1974–* .

Continuation of # 33 in book form; since 1983 issued on microfiche. Large portion of *NUC* available in MARC database.

35. *New Serial Titles, 1950–70: A Union List of Serials Commencing Publication after December 31, 1949.* Washington: Library of Congress, 1973. 4 vols. Updates: *1971–75* (1976), 2 vols; *1976–80* (1981), 2 vols; *1981–85* (1986), 6 vols; *1986–89* (1990), 6 vols.

36. *Union List of Serials in Libraries of the United States and Canada.* 3rd ed, NY: Wilson, 1965. 5 vols.

Limited by age, but best listing of major libraries' holdings of journals that began before 1950.

37. *United States Catalog: Books in Print.* NY: Wilson, 1899–1928. 4 vols, 7 supplements.

Periodic cumulation from publishers' catalogues, arranged by author, title & subject. Continued by *CBI* (# 30).

38. *United States Newspaper Program National Union List.* 3rd ed, Dublin, Ohio: OCLC, 1989.

Ongoing cooperative listing of all library holdings, with locations & exact holdings, both paper & microfilm.

INDEXES TO PRIMARY SOURCES

39. *Reader's Guide to Periodical Literature: An Author and Subject Index.* NY: Wilson, 1900– . Monthly, with quarterly & annual cumulations. †
Guide to popular, nontechnical magazines.

40. *Short Story Index: An Index to Stories in Collections and Periodicals.* NY: Wilson, 1953– . Annual, periodic cumulations.

BIBLIOGRAPHIES OF CRITICISM

41. *The American Novel 1789–1959: A Checklist of Twentieth-Century Criticism* by Donna L Gerstenberger & George Hendrick. Denver: Swallow, 1961. *Volume II: Criticism Written 1960–1968.* Chicago: Swallow, 1970.

Listing by novelist & by novel. Good starting point.

42. *American Short-Fiction Criticism and Scholarship, 1959–1977: A Checklist* by Joe Weixlmann. Chicago: Swallow, 1982.
    Comprehensive, accurate & usable.
43. *Articles on Twentieth-Century Literature: An Annotated Bibliography, 1954–70,* ed David E Pownall. Millwood, NY: Kraus, 1973–1980. 7 vols.
    International in scope of subjects & journals indexed.
44. *The Contemporary Novel: A Checklist of Critical Literature on the British and American Novel Since 1945* by Irving Adelman & Rita Dworkin. Metuchen, NJ: Scarecrow, 1972.
    Criticism of 200 authors, listed by novelist & novel.
45. *Literary History of the United States: Bibliography.* 4th ed, ed Robert E Spiller et al. NY: Macmillan/London: Collier Macmillan, 1974.
    Awkward but important combination of three previously published bibliographies covering pre-1948, 1948–1958, 1958–1970. See # 17.
46. *Short Fiction Criticism: A Checklist of Interpretation Since 1925 of Stories and Novelettes (American, British, Continental), 1800–1958,* ed Jarvis Thurston et al. Denver: Swallow, 1960.
    Useful for early criticism; updated by Weixlmann (#42).
47. *Sixteen Modern American Authors: A Survey of Research and Criticism,* ed Jackson R Bryer. Durham, NC: Duke U P, rev 1974. Vol 2 (1989) covers 1972–1988.
    S Anderson, Cather, S Crane, Dreiser, Eliot, Faulkner, Fitzgerald, Frost, Hemingway, O'Neill, Pound, Robinson, Steinbeck, Stevens, W C Williams & Wolfe.
48. *Twentieth-Century Short Story Explication, 1900–1975* by Warren S Walker. 3rd ed, Hamden, Conn: Shoe String, 1977. Supplements, *1976–1978* (1980), *1977–1981* (1984), *1981–1984* (1987), *1984–1986* (1989), *1987–1988* (1991). Index (1992).
    Extensive, but difficult to use. Journal abbreviations defined in supplements.

PERIODICAL GUIDES TO CRITICISM

49. *Abstracts of English Studies.* Calgary: U Calgary P, 1958– . Quarterly.
    International guide of articles & essays, many not indexed elsewhere, on English & American literature.
50. *American Literary Scholarship.* Durham, NC: Duke U P, 1965– . Annual.
    Bibliographic essays on genres, authors, periods.
51. *Annual Bibliography of English Language and Literature.* Cambridge, UK: Modern Humanities Research Association, 1920– . Annual.
    International, arranged by topic. Supplements *MLAIB* (#57).

52. *Book Review Digest.* NY: Wilson, 1905– . 10 times per year, cumulated annually. †

Excerpts from reviews of popular books in magazines & newspapers.

53. *Book Review Index.* Detroit: Gale, 1965– . Bimonthly, cumulated. †

Far more comprehensive than #52; especially good for scholarly books & novels receiving limited attention.

54. *Combined Retrospective Index to Book Reviews in Humanities Journals, 1802–1974.* Woodbridge, Conn: Research Publications, 1982–1984. 10 vols.

500,000 reviews from 150 journals listed; especially strong in literature.

55. *Contemporary Literary Criticism: Excerpts From the Criticism of Today's Novelists, Poets, Playwrights and Other Creative Writers.* Detroit: Gale, 1973– .

International coverage, long excerpts from criticism. Format similar to *TCLC* (#58).

56. *Humanities Index.* NY: Wilson, 1974– . Quarterly, cumulated annually.

Not as comprehensive as *MLAIB* (#57), but interdisciplinary, covering history, philosophy, theology, as well as language & literature. Valuable for timeliness. Supersedes *International Index* (1907–1965) & *Social Sciences and Humanities Index* (1965–1974).

57. *MLA International Bibliography of Books and Articles on the Modern Languages and Literature.* NY: MLA, 1921– . Annual. †

Extensive, international coverage of American literature & since 1981 enhanced by subject index. Arrangement by nationality & period. Must be supplemented by other indexes.

58. *Twentieth-Century Literary Criticism: Excerpts From Criticism of the Works of Novelists, Poets, Playwrights, Short Story Writers, and Other Creative Writers, 1900–1960, From the First Published Critical Appraisals to Current Evaluations.* Detroit: Gale, 1978– .

GUIDES TO RESEARCH

59. *Bibliographical Guide to the Study of the Literature of the U.S.A.* by Clarence L Gohdes & Sanford E Marovitz. 5th ed, Durham, NC: Duke U P, 1984.

Annotated listing, especially good for topical approach.

60. *Literary Research Guide: A Guide to Reference Sources for the Study of Literatures in English and Related Topics* by James L Harner. NY: MLA, 1989.

Useful manual for using the library. Hundreds of annotations on selected reference books; appendixes.

61. *The Book in America: A History of the Making and Selling of Books in the United States* by Hellmut Lehmann-Haupt et al. 2nd ed, NY: Bowker, 1952.
62. *Glaister's Glossary of the Book* by Geoffrey Ashall Glaister. 2nd ed, London: Allen & Unwin, 1979.
    Treats all aspects of the book & publishing. Illustrations & appendixes.
63. *Guide to the Study of United States Imprints* by G Thomas Tanselle. Cambridge: Harvard U P, 1971. 2 vols.
    Comprehensive checklists of materials on all aspects of printing & publishing history. See also *DLB* (#25), vol 46.
64. *A History of American Magazines* by Frank Luther Mott. Cambridge: Harvard U P, 1938–1968. 5 vols.
    Covers 1741–1930, by period, genre & specific titles.
65. *History of Book Publishing in the United States* by John W Tebbel. NY: Bowker, 1973–1981. 4 vols.

DIRECTORIES

66. *Literary Market Place: The Directory of American Book Publishing.* NY: Bowker, 1940– . Annual.
    Addresses & information for publishers, agents, reviewers, book clubs, etc.
67. *MLA Directory of Periodicals: A Guide to Journals and Series in Languages and Literatures.* NY: MLA, 1979– . Annual.
    Listing of all serials indexed by *MLAIB* (#57).
68. *Ulrich's International Periodicals Directory.* NY: Bowker, 1932– . Annual.
    Best listing of currently published titles by subject; valuable for listing of indexes that cover each journal.

Important Journals

J-1. *American Literature: A Journal of Literary History, Criticism, and Bibliography.* Durham, NC: Duke U P, 1929– . Quarterly.
    Critical articles, book reviews, research in progress; formerly thorough, now selective bibliography.
J-2. *American Quarterly.* Philadelphia: U Pennsylvania P, 1949– . Quarterly.
    Explores the cultural background of literature. Bibliographical essays.
J-3. *Modern Fiction Studies.* West Lafayette, Ind: Purdue U, Department of English, 1955– . Quarterly.

A CHECKLIST FOR STUDENTS OF AMERICAN FICTION   89

J-4. *Resources for American Literary Study*. College Park: U Maryland, Department of English, 1971– . Semiannual.

J-5. *Studies in American Fiction*. Boston: Northeastern U, Department of English, 1973– . Semiannual.

— Daniel Boice

COMPUTER AVAILABILITY

Reference works for American fiction are increasingly available through computer technology. Some are accessible on CD-ROM or on computerized catalogues of large libraries. Others are "on-line" tools, which are used via telephone linkage to computer centers or data bases. More and more tools can be used in several of these formats, and reference librarians can advise on which tools are available at individual libraries.

Advantages of computerized resources include speed, ability to look for several topics at once, and printing out of citations. Factors that determine the usefulness of these tools include the reliability of both data and method, ease of use, and especially scope—that is, how broadly the tool covers the subject and what years and journals it indexes. Many computerized tools cover only recent years and must be supplemented by using printed versions.

Titles in the Checklist that are at least partially available by computer are marked by daggers (†). Reference librarians will be able to provide advice and direction. Other major computer tools include:

OCLC (Online Computer Library Center): A network including nearly all American libraries and many foreign ones. Lists millions of books, journals, maps, recordings and archival materials. Especially useful for identifying libraries with specific titles.

RLIN (Research Libraries Network): Listing of items held by the leading American research libraries, the Research Libraries Group. Good for all library materials, especially archives.

Both the *OCLC* and *RLIN* databases include the recent Library of Congress cataloguing, called *MARC* (Machine Readable Cataloguing). The strength of *OCLC* is its broad coverage of libraries, but *RLIN* is more careful in its cataloguing. Both *RLIN* and *OCLC* offer several ways to locate books, beyond the traditional avenues of author and title. Librarians will provide information regarding availability of these tools.

— *Daniel Boice*

MODERN CLASSIC WRITERS:
Basic Literary Histories

Bradbury, Malcolm. *The Modern American Novel*. NY: Oxford U P, 1984.

Cowley, Malcolm. *A Second Flowering: Works and Days of the Lost Generation*. NY: Viking, 1973.

Eisinger, Chester E. *Fiction of the Forties*. Chicago: U Chicago P, 1963.

Hoffman, Frederick J. *The Twenties: American Writing in the Postwar Decade*. NY: Collier, rev 1962.

Karl, Frederick. *American Fiction, 1940–1980: A Comprehensive History and Critical Evaluation*. NY: Harper & Row, 1983.

Kimbel, Bobby Ellen, ed. *Dictionary of Literary Biography, Volume One-Hundred Two: American Short-Story Writers, 1910–1945*. Detroit: Bruccoli Clark Layman/Gale, 1991.

Kolb, Harold H, Jr. *A Field Guide to the Study of American Literature*. Charlottesville: U P Virginia, 1976.

Martine, James J, ed. *Dictionary of Literary Biography, Volume Nine: American Novelists, 1910–1945*. Detroit: Bruccoli Clark Layman/Gale, 1981. 3 vols.

Peden, William. *The American Short Story: Continuity and Change, 1940–1975*. 2nd ed, Boston: Houghton Mifflin, 1975.

Stevick, Philip, ed. *The American Short Story, 1900–1945: A Critical History*. Boston: Twayne, 1984.

Thorp, Willard. *American Writing in the Twentieth Century*. Cambridge: Harvard U P, 1960.

Weaver, Gordon, ed. *The American Short Story, 1945–1980: A Critical History*. Boston: Twayne, 1983.

— Daniel Boice

INDEX

Writers' names appear in **boldface.**

F

Fable, A (William Faulkner) 1, 3, 6, 8, 15, 18
Farewell to Arms, A (Ernest Hemingway) 31, 34, 41–42, 45, 47
Father Abraham (William Faulkner) (ed. James B. Meriwether) 4
Faulkner: A Collection of Critical Essays (ed. Robert Penn Warren) 64
Faulkner, William viii, ix, 1–20
  bibliographies and catalogues 1–2
  biographies
    books 6–7
    book sections 7
  concordances 5–6
  critical studies
    articles 13–20
    books 8–10
    book sections 11–13
    essay collections 10–11
    special journals 11
  interviews 7–8
  writings by
    books 2–4
    editions and collections 5
    letters 4–5
    manuscripts and archives 5
Faulkner's County: Tales of Yoknapatawpha County 3
Faulkner's MGM Screenplays (ed. Bruce F. Kawin) 4
Faulkner's University Pieces (ed. Carvel Collins) 3
Fiesta (Ernest Hemingway) 34
Fifth Column, The (Ernest Hemingway) 34, 40
Fifth Column and Four Stories of the Spanish Civil War, The (Ernest Hemingway) 35
Fifth Column and the First Forty-nine Stories, The (Ernest Hemingway) 34
Fitzgerald, F. Scott viii, ix, 21–32
  bibliographies 21
  biographies
    articles 25–26
    books 24–25
    book sections 25
  concordances 24
  critical studies
    articles 29–32
    books 26–27
    book sections 28–29
    essay collections 27–28
    special journals 28
  writings by
    books 21–22
    collections 23–24
    editions and collections 24
    letters, diaries, and notebooks 23
    manuscripts and archives 24
Flags in the Dust (William Faulkner) (ed. Douglas Day) 3, 16
Flappers and Philosophers (F. Scott Fitzgerald) 21
Flood: A Romance of Our Time (Robert Penn Warren) 62, 68, 71
Forgotten Village, The (John Steinbeck) 49
For Whom the Bell Tolls (Ernest Hemingway) 34, 42–43
From Death to Morning (Thomas Wolfe) 73
Frost, Robert ix
F. Scott Fitzgerald Manuscripts (ed. Matthew J. Bruccoli) 22
F. Scott Fitzgerald's Preface to This Side of Paradise (ed. John R. Hopkins) 22
F. Scott Fitzgerald's Screenplay for Three Comrades (ed. Matthew J. Bruccoli) 22
F. Scott Fitzgerald's St. Paul Plays, 1911–1914 (ed. Alan Margolies) 22

G

Garden of Eden, The (Ernest Hemingway) 35, 47
Gentlemen of the Press (Thomas Wolfe) 74
Ghosts of Rowan Oak, The: William Faulkner's Ghost Stories for Children (recounted by Dean Faulkner Wells) 4
Go Down, Moses (William Faulkner) 3, 5, 19
God Rest You Merry Gentlemen (Ernest Hemingway) 34
Gods of Mount Olympus, The (Robert Penn Warren) 62
Good Child's River, The (Thomas Wolfe) (ed. Suzanne Stutman) 74
Grapes of Wrath, The (John Steinbeck) 48–59
Great Gatsby, The (F. Scott Fitzgerald) 22, 24, 26–31
Green Bough, A (William Faulkner) 3
Green Hills of Africa (Ernest Hemingway) 34, 45, 47

H

Hamlet, The (William Faulkner) 3, 6, 16–19
Harvard University (Cambridge, Massachusetts) 75
Harvest Gypsies, The: On the Road to The Grapes of Wrath (John Steinbeck) 50
Helen: A Courtship (William Faulkner) 4
Hemingway, Ernest viii, ix, x–xi, 33–47
  bibliographies and catalogues 33–34

U

Uncollected Stories (William Faulkner) (ed. Joseph Blotner) 4, 6
Uncollected Stories of John Steinbeck (ed. Kiyoshi Nakayama) 50
Unvanquished, The (William Faulkner) 3

V

Vanderbilt University (Nashville, Tennessee) 64
Vegetable, The: or, From President to Postman (F. Scott Fitzgerald) 22
Virginia, University of (Charlottesville) 5, 36
Vision in Spring (William Faulkner) (ed. Judith Sensibar) 4
Viva Zapata! (John Steinbeck) (ed. Robert E. Morsberger) 50

W

Warren, Robert Penn 61–72
  bibliographies 61
  biographies
    articles 64–65
    books 64
  critical studies
    articles 68–72
    books 66
    book sections 67–68
    essay collections 66–67
    special journals 67
  interviews
    articles 65–66
    books 65
    book sections 65
  writings by
    books 61–63
    collections 64
    manuscripts and archives 64
"Was" (William Faulkner) 17
Wayward Bus, The (John Steinbeck) 49
Web and the Rock, The (Thomas Wolfe) 73–74
Welcome to Our City (Thomas Wolfe) (ed. Richard S. Kennedy) 74
Western Kentucky University (Bowling Green) 64
"White Quail, The" (John Steinbeck) 59
Whittier, John Greenleaf 64
Who Speaks for the Negro? (Robert Penn Warren) 62

Wilderness: A Tale of the Civil War (Robert Penn Warren) 62, 72
Wild Palms, The (William Faulkner) 3, 6, 9, 18
Wild Years, The (Ernest Hemingway) (ed. Gene Z. Hanrahan) 35
William Faulkner Manuscripts (eds. Joseph Blotner, Thomas L. McHaney) 4
Winner Take Nothing (Ernest Hemingway) 34
Winter of Our Discontent, The (John Steinbeck) 50, 57
Wishing Tree, The (William Faulkner) 3
Wolfe, Thomas viii, ix, 73–81
  bibliographies 73
  biographies
    articles 76–77
    books 76
    book sections 76
  critical studies
    articles 79–81
    books 77–78
    book sections 78–79
    essay collections 78
    special journals 78
  interviews 77
  writings by
    books 73–74
    collections 75
    letters, diaries, and notebooks 74–75
    manuscripts and archives 75
World Enough and Time: A Romantic Novel (Robert Penn Warren) 62, 68–70
World War I (1914–1918) viii
writings
  Faulkner 2–5
  Fitzgerald 21–24
  Hemingway 34–36
  Steinbeck 49–51
  Warren 61–64
  Wolfe 73–75

Y

Yale University (New Haven, Connecticut) 64
You, Emperors, and Others: Poems, 1957–1960 (Robert Penn Warren) 62
You Can't Go Home Again (Thomas Wolfe) 73–74

Z

Zapata, the Little Tiger (John Steinbeck) 50